The Desi Divorcee

INSPIRING TRUE STORIES OF INDIAN WOMEN SURVIVING AND THRIVING AFTER DIVORCE

Jessie Arora

Sharan Bilan

Devangini Mahapatra Chauhan

Noopura Huddar

Misriya Jacksi

Preet Johal

Loveleen Kaur

Manny Kaur

Sabrina Kaur

Deepika Sandhu

Matina Singh

Priya Kaur Tahim

FOREWORD BY SUKHI DHILLON
EPILOGUE BY SHILPA CACHO

Soul sparks PRESS

soulsparkspress.com

Co-editors Deepika Sandhu and Devangini Mahapatra Chauhan
Cover design by Adam Donshik
Book design and production by Little Men Roaring, LLC

ISBN: 979-8-218-57489-5 (Paperback)
ISBN: 979-8-9922748-2-0 (Kindle)

CONTENTS

NOTE TO READER

This book contains depictions of domestic abuse, suicidal ideation, and sexual assault. There are also mentions of substance abuse, childhood trauma, mental health issues and alcohol addiction. If you feel this kind of content may be triggering, read with care.

RESOURCES

FOR DOMESTIC ABUSE:

https://www.domesticshelters.org
National Domestic shelter directory

https://www.manavi.org/
South Asian non-profit

SEXUAL ASSAULT:

https://www.nsvrc.org/
National resource with tools and information

https://sakhi.org/sexual-assault-program/
South Asian based in NYC

SUBSTANCE ABUSE/HEALTH SERVICES:

https://www.samhsa.gov/find-help

MENTAL HEALTH SERVICES:

https://southasiantherapists.org/

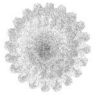

FOREWORD

Growing up, desi women like myself felt pressured to marry by a certain age. Not only was it a parental expectation, it was a social one too. The community would often gossip about women who were getting too old to marry, or those who dared to focus on their careers rather than find a suitable life partner. Marriage allowed our parents to hold their heads up high, as it raised their status in the community, and gave them bragging rights too. It was almost as if our parents could finally say, "See, there's nothing wrong with my daughter. She is marriage material!"

Unfortunately, our community still believes that a woman's worth is tied to her marriage status. Patriarchy groomed women for marriage and this is one reason why we think that women "must be married." She can be a CEO, own several properties, or be financially independent, yet none of her self-accomplishments come close to marriage; being married is seen as the ultimate goal in life.

But what happens when that marriage breaks down and ends in divorce? How does the community come to her aid?

The divorced lifestyle challenges our traditional norms; our society upholds a nuclear marriage or even better, the daughter-in-law moving into her in-laws home. two-parent family as the norm. Anything outside of that is stigmatized. But this social stigma (when the public has prejudices against a stigmatized group) often leads to a self-stigma (when a person internalizes stereotypes about themselves and their situation). And there are higher levels of self-stigma among divorced and single-parent women, which negatively impacts their willingness to seek help, accept support, or engage in psychological interventions. And that can lead to a downward spiral.

And that's where this book, "The Desi Divorcee" comes in.

Reading incredible true stories, like those in this book by brave authors who have endured it all only to survive and thrive is absolutely needed in our community. Their stories may be detailed and tragic, but they offer inspiration to help women who are going through a turbulent or traumatic partnership. A woman will always think, "It can't be that bad, others have it worse. I can't justify leaving him," until they read about others and compare how bad it really is. These stories offer a different view. What these courageous desi divorcees have done is truthfully and openly shared their stories so you can feel a sense of connection, belonging, support and your own courage in your own heart to take the path that is best for you.

As a community, we are not doing enough to help women. Divorce is not the be-all end-all that our family thinks it is, and the notion that a woman should stick with the marriage "no matter what" will only kill our sisters. Instead of isolating or shunning these women, we need to believe them, trust them when they confide in us and help them get out. A woman should not have to feel guilt, shame, or embarrassment for going through an unsuccessful marriage; a lot of that comes from our community judging her. The only way we can slowly remove the stigma associated with divorce is to normalize divorce and talk about it openly.

We need to reframe divorce as a chapter in someone's life, or for some, a challenging life experience that leads to a new journey. Women should not be defined by their marriage status or the adjective society slaps on them; let their powerful yet vulnerable words do that.

Let's break the cycle for these women and our future daughters.

~Sukhi

Sukhi is a social media influencer, community activist and college professor who speaks openly about breaking down stereotypes and prejudices in the South Asian Community, particularly amongst the Punjabi Sikh diaspora. Through her courage and story telling Sukhi is thoughtfully challenging stereotypes and prejudices while teaching others about her religion. Her recent viral "Cycle Breaking" series was showcased at the ISAFFC and tackles taboo subjects in a thought-provoking and courageous way. You can find Sukhi on social media as OneSikhMom.

Introduction From the Co-Editor
DEEPIKA SANDHU

Hello Friend,

I couldn't believe the stories I was hearing.

Forty women in 10 days responded to our call for stories about their Indian divorce.

Women from all different parts of the world.

Women with all different stories.

Stories of abuse, addiction, deep sadness and shame.

Each story was different, but there was one common theme.

They felt alone.

Despite South Asian culture advancing and progressing in so many ways, the idea of being a divorcee in a community that upholds marriage as a bastion of honor felt daunting and isolating, as if they were the only samosa lost in a donut shop.

One recently divorced woman said to me, "I felt so alone and confused at the start of my divorce that I Googled 'Do Indian girls get divorced?' Nothing came up that would help me. It made me feel even more alone."

This book is here to change that.

Twelve beautiful humans have taken the brave step to share their stories with the world in the hopes of giving other women just like you the courage, the support, and the confidence to move forward in their own lives.

Divorcing wasn't the end for any of us.

It was a new beginning, a new chapter, a new phase of life that took all of us from desperate, heartbroken, confused and unsure to new lives full of courage, confidence, and the strength to move forward in our truth.

And it will be for you too.

No more playing small.

No more living for others and not for yourself.

No more accepting less than you desire and deserve.

It's time to confidently, courageously and completely be all of YOU.

Our twelve stories are here to cheer you on.

Always,

Deepika

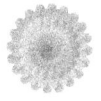

Introduction From the Co-Editor
DEVANGINI MAHAPATRA CHAUHAN

Dear Husband, In Laws, Society, Etc,

When I married and entered your home, I was somehow convinced that I had made it in life, but that could not have been further from the truth. Because the truth is simple – my life is not just my marriage.

Yes, you heard me. And yes, I know it's a difficult one to gulp. But guess what, you can get through this too. Just follow my lead. Take a sip of your tea and repeat after me – this is not the end of the world; we do not care what people think; she did not enter our home to serve us and take our bloodline forward.

I am allowed to move on and I do not need your permission. And it can be done amicably with mutual consent. Ask the Supreme Court of India if you do not believe me.

Sincerely,

Not Your Property Anymore

It had all started with this letter. I remember growing up and wondering why girls were taught one thing, and boys were taught something else. Upon questioning, I mostly received gasps and looks that conveyed doom. I was told by many people that I would wind up divorced and discarded for this attitude.

Luckily, my parents were of a slightly different school of thought. As their parents had been. I was told very clearly that physical abuse, alcoholism, cheating and financial abuse were not to be tolerated. In time, my family has learned to add emotional abuse and toxicity to this mix. I was told that even one instance must lead to only one outcome – a ticket for a flight or train back home. Even on my wedding day, they emphasized on the fact that the doors to their home would always be open for me—that their home would always remain mine, too. That I had not merely been brought up to get married and stay married – whatever the cost might be.

But many girls in Southeast Asia are not given this privilege. It was during my divorce that I realized I had been blessed with a privileged upbringing. There were so many women who came up to me and congratulated me on my courage because apparently, at the time, it was unthinkable to walk out without falling into a deep black hole filled with the tar of taboo.

This was merely 10 years ago. To my mind, the emotional and financial repercussions of going through separation and divorce are larger and more pressing challenges that one needs to address. Yet, in our culture, it is the finger pointing that women have been most focused on.

What will society say?

What will people say?

What if their children are ostracized and branded as children from a broken home?

To me, all of this looked like a broken society.

Just like the broken concept of marriage that I had been immersed in. I was trying to adhere to the law of the Great Indian Marriage, where the girl is treated like a piece of property, merely an exchanging of hands, rather than the precious gem that is being lovingly sent to create an entire world and new generation for another family. I did not see the abuse I faced as a personal one – I saw it as an abuse of the core Indian values that my ancestors had established since ancient times.

And these values did not align with the deep and beautiful knowledge that had been handed to me by my grandmothers and great-grandmothers. These women had always told me one thing very clearly, "Under no circumstances will you hand over your feminine identity to someone – because no home can be built on the shoulders of a broken woman who does not know to stand up for herself. You will not do that to the upcoming generations."

So, for their sake, I have taken my broken pieces, and built a life that I am proud of. One where I am a hands-on mother to a daughter with solid goals in life. One where I am an award-winning publisher who started her business from scratch. One where I am a bestselling author and well-loved book coach who uses her spirituality and mental wellness practice to coax stories out of people—to give purpose to many others.

That is my identity.

I want any Southeast Asian woman reading this to know that she is not her broken marriage. She is the courage she showed in walking out and choosing something better for herself. She is the promise she has made to her future generations by walking out and breaking generational curses.

And I am so proud of you.

This book is a guide and a gift, and the outpourings of 12 women who courageously show us what lies beyond the fear of leaving.

Because I Didn't Blink

DEVANGINI MAHAPATRA CHAUHAN

"Why are you sad? You chose to get divorced. So, you should be happy."

I wanted to ask; if you decided to stay in your marriage despite the daily strife your children see—a marriage that you wear like a badge of honor—how come you aren't happy?

Instead, I listened to the person at the other end of the phone—a family member, no less. I knew there was something very toxic about that statement—because that's what it was. It may have been posed as a question, but it was a statement that left no room at all for my side of the story.

Which is why the story of divorce—especially in India—must change, I decided then and there. But for that to happen, first it must be told without any shame.

And even though the question came from a very toxic place, it did not change the fact that this is probably what I would be facing from here on.

Was I ready to let this become my identity? Would this be my new name? Divorced? Devangini Divorced? Devangini Damaged? Devangini Selfish? Devangini Failure? Devangini Unfit Parent? Devangini Sullied Wife? Victim Who was once a Chauhan? Devangini—what?

Would I not be known for the business I had effortlessly yet tirelessly worked to set up? For the conviction with which I had given our child a better quality of life than even the father had admitted he couldn't? Or for the awards I had won, the media coverage my work had garnered—all in just 5 years? The fact that I had found the grace and courage to separate the toxic abusive ex-husband from the father to keep said father in the child's life—even if it meant showing up for weekend visits and video calls alongside my daughter to give her a sense of the happier family we had become, to teach her to not just give up on people entirely? Would these things never matter in the larger picture?

What would my identity be now?

Identity.

The word made me go back a few months in time.

The courthouse had been dusty and busy, as was mandatory with most government buildings in India. The Family Court, it proudly proclaimed outside. Inside, there were families disintegrating under the pressure of broken marriages. A dam of emotions was being held within each person standing there, while a reservoir of strength was in constant demand.

I stood there before a judge, being asked to sign my name on a petition that would put our mutual consent divorce in motion.

Apparently we had finally managed to agree on something. Mutually.

As I picked up the pen, surrounded by people who were busy making their own noise heard above the red-tapism that snaked through these hallowed halls, my ears went deaf. My senses were silent. My mind was blank. My hands were numb, as if hitting my fists against the stone wall of his abuse had finally taken its toll on me.

The pages in front of me, the ones I was stooped over, suddenly looked blurry. I wasn't sure what was happening. As I swiped the back of my hand against my eyes to ease the blurriness, I found the salty wetness of uninvited tears. My mind finally formed its first coherent thought, and I looked up, completely confused. The lawyer and my soon-to-be ex-husband both looked at me, a little concerned and most definitely annoyed.

"What's wrong?" the lawyer asked gently.

"What name do I sign here? My married last name or my maiden name?"

It had all started with my name. And it all ended there.

I did not know it when I was signing those papers, but my brain was trying to escape the clutches of what would now be a lifelong memory, a trigger for lifelong grief. I was trying to clutch aimlessly at the raft of the most random thought, refusing to let go, refusing to even look back at the large sinking ship that I had just jumped from.

What happened to an Indian woman when she got divorced? What happened when she was not Mrs. Chauhan, the one whose new identity had been forged when she took those seven rounds around the sacred fire? What happened when she was not to be someone's wife, when she was not to be what she had been brought up to be?

They had told her how to be a good wife, a good mother, a good daughter-in-law, a good sister-in-law. And it had all involved becoming that new last name. No one had told her how to be a good divorcee. All I had been told was that it was bad to be a divorcee. Is that why there was no template for it? Who were you if you were not someone's wife – would you go back to being your father's daughter? Would the shame let you wear another identity with pride?

Could that marital identity be reversed? With one signature? Could we go back on the sacred vows? Would the Heavens and the Gods allow that? Could a court dissolve what the Gods had been summoned to decree, witness, and bless?

"You are a Chauhan now—only a Chauhan. No more Mahapatra-Shahapatra now. So leave that in the past now."

I remember hearing these words very early on in my marriage—from my in-laws. The memory makes me shudder. There was a silent threat in those words – even though they came from a loving family. A little dry, but very loving. And when I tried to tell the husband how uncomfortable this line had made me—especially because it came from people I had barely met in my life – he dismissed me by saying, "Well, that's how they are showing you their love and accepting you in their lives."

That did not make me feel better. No one had taught me to see these comments as inappropriate or how to address my feelings around them. So, I allowed him to shame me into thinking I was being a bad wife by doubting the intention behind the comments. If being Mrs. Chauhan meant I was to be their property, I could give them that. Without thinking too much about it. If earning their love meant letting these things go, I could do it without much thought. If they gave me love, I could forgive them and justify these comments.

Without thinking about myself.

Apparently, it was so rare to have in-laws who gave love—any love—and respect, I was willing to let go of anything that did not sit well with me. Plus, growing up, I had only been taught that I could hand in my walking papers if my husband:

1. Hit me
2. Cheated on me
3. Drank excessively
4. Did not support me financially

No one had thought to add emotional abuse, gaslighting, and manipulation to the list. No one had thought to add sneaking in medication meant for patients of depression to the list. No one had added acts like recording my frustration during a fight to blackmail me later to the list. So I did not add these things either. It was a different story that he did all of the above and then some during the course of our courtship and marriage, while I stayed on and screamed like a bludgeoned woman to get him to behave. Instead of leaving and taking my expectations to a saner place to a home where I would be safe. One that I would build for myself. Because I didn't know I could do that. That I could have a home or identity of my own.

Very soon, these comments of 'belongingness' were followed up with, "Now that you are married, we come first, then your husband, and then your family." Also, "Now that you are married, you will have to ensure you do not spend his money and make sure you save it so that you can help us buy property. In fact, when will you start to earn?" And very often, "Why does your family need you? We can't give you more than the usual annual leave."

I had not thought it would be a competition. And it was scary to think that I had to renounce my parents—because if I did not have a home to go back to in case things went south, where would that leave me? At their mercy?

It may not have been scary if my husband did not defend them by saying they only wanted what was best for our financial future and that I must listen to them and hand over my income to him and his brother—it wasn't as if they were asking for a dowry! It may not have been scary if I had not believed them when they said they were doing me a favor by showing me the armed forces. Yes, this husband of mine was an officer of the Indian Army. As were all the men of his family.

It may not have been so scary if I hadn't watched how his elder brother's marriage was disintegrating right before my eyes. And how they openly talked about how "unfortunate" it was that her parents were letting her come back home, sheltering this oh-so-terrible behavior of her choosing herself. Because what greater good was there than letting yourself become a martyr who had to make a marriage work at all costs?

It may not have been so scary if I didn't know in my heart that I too had done something wrong. To escape a narcissistic home, I had chosen the biggest red flag of a guy. And I had gone from one prison to another.

So, technically, yes, I was at their mercy.

Well, that's precisely how it began.

I was left in Palampur—a tiny town in the foothills of the Himalayas in Himachal Pradesh—a few weeks after the wedding. Correction: a few weeks, and a botched honeymoon later.

And that set the tone for the rest of my marriage.

I personally saw to it that there was no other tone allowed to set in. I refused to speak up, I refused to address what was bothering me, I refused to confront any red flags, and I refused to ask for better conditions, because I did not want to be sent back. I did not yet know that I could build a life for myself.

So, when I did finally speak up, it came as such a jarring shock to him that he promptly asked me to leave. Several times. Yet, I could not. There was so much more to my story, I was convinced. I was not ready to give up.

I have tried to write my story several times, and I have also tried very hard not to write it. Because honestly, even though his parents gave me all the love they could—far more than their culture and conditioning allowed them to, and from some magnanimity of their hearts that came from within and certainly not the stifling culture of the village they hailed from—they also showed me every red flag that a girl should be warned about. This is also the only reason that warranted writing my story. I want to be kind to them and give my disclaimer here—they were not the problem. The mindset they were trapped in is what I need to address—the limits that were given to them by problematic conditioning. If left up to them, they would have done everything in their power to keep me happy. But I did not open my mouth because I did not want to put them in a position to have to choose between all they knew, however limited, and me. I let them choose their comfort zone, silently.

Which is why it was easy for the iron woman, my mother-in-law, to say, "If he hit you, then you must have done something to deserve it." The woman I respected so much showed her loyalty to that last name—a last name that apparently subjugated a good woman in the name of *Rajput* values. That day she gifted me a vital lesson in making your identity by choice, and not as a side effect of marriage. She taught me what kind of *Rajput* warrior I must teach my daughter to be—an authentic one like this lady almost was, not the garden-variety version she was trying to adhere to. So I forgave her.

Their son, though—a whole other story. I could not excuse him because he did not grow up in the village. He grew up in the hallowed halls of the prestigious Indian armed forces, and he became a very fine, righteous officer himself. So, I have no explanation for him being more of a monster and less of a husband during our marriage. The only way to describe him as a husband is toxic and abusive. The only way to describe his parents is limited by their culture and lack of exposure. Them, I can forgive. Him, I will never understand. Except that the trauma of being told from a young age to "be a man" gave him enough baggage to use as aggression with his wife when he thought no one was watching.

And then refusing to take his medications which were prescribed to him for clinical aggression.

Because men, apparently, don't cry.

About seven years into our marriage, or whatever our arrangement might be called, I had to renew my passport and apply for our child's passport as well. My family lived abroad, and I would always need to have a valid visa and passport. This was the very opportunity he needed.

"Why must you be Devangini Mahapatra Chauhan now? Why must the Mahapatra stay?"

I sighed. I did not want to get into this discussion again. From experience, I knew that there was only one reason he was asking me this question again—to intimidate me, to make me feel ridiculous when asked to explain it again and again, to reduce my reason to a feeble, laughable pile of nonsense that needed to be dismissed. To let me know that if I didn't stop answering, I would be dismissed. Possibly with violence. And of course, I was asked in front of the child so that getting irritated or getting into a fight would then be used as the main issue—one that made me a screaming shrew who needed to be tamed.

It had always been this way. They had always been insecure about me holding on to my identity. There had always been a few subtle taunts from his elder brother (yes, the very one who had driven his wife to insanity) about how I was from a higher caste and should not be allowed to let them feel inferior (never my agenda, but somehow always my crime).

Even when we bought property soon after our marriage and the sale deed said Devangini Mahapatra, because that's what my passport at the time said, there had been a considerable debate about how inappropriate it was. His brother was the one to plant this poisonous seed in everyone's head.

And now, here he was—his brother's minion—acting like the man his brother always accused him of not being. By trying to subdue me, threaten me and take my identity as some sort of trophy, the spoils of war. Because marriage to him was a raging battle that he had to win at all costs.

"I will give you the documents for the residence proof only if you change your name to Chauhan."

"Sure," I said as I fed our two-year-old daughter, "Devangini Mahapatra Chauhan—I am looking forward to adding the Chauhan."

"No, you need to drop the Mahapatra."

"I can't be both?"

"No."

I wanted to remind him that I had been educated and exposed to high standards by my Mahapatra parents, which had helped me perform exceptionally well as Mrs. Chauhan in the army, elevating him from the back bench, where he always found solace, to the spotlight that he very firmly deserved. This officer was dedicated to his troops in a way that made him the perfect officer, the perfect leader. Yet, I knew this would lead to a fight—it went against his manhood to be reminded that I had always gone above and beyond my duty, earning us much fame in every single military station. I was expected to do this work without talking about it. Because being a man also meant his ego was very delicate. If anything, his parents and brother had been very visibly worried when he had praised me and bragged about how much every Army General's wife wanted me for their events.

"Keep criticizing her so that she does more. Don't praise her; she will dance on your head and reduce you to a henpecked, non-man." My in-laws kept drumming the point home.

So, there I was, tired and frustrated. And a little scared. What if I did not get a passport? Did that mean I would not get to leave and go where my people were? His family had already ensured that he did not get a passport so that I could not "take him away to America." What if they tried to keep me and my daughter here too?

That same afternoon, while he sat in his air-conditioned office, with the car I was not allowed to touch (bought with my earnings) parked outside, I took an auto-rickshaw in the Delhi heat with my child and went to see a lawyer who could file for the cumbersome name change process so that I could get myself and my child a passport. As Mrs. Chauhan.

And now, I was being asked to give up that surname.

So, who am I supposed to be? At least he used to fight with me for that name. I used to fight back because he meant something to me, and hence I wanted things a certain way with him in my life. Now that he was leaving, what was my life to be?

What was my name supposed to be?

I would find out soon, but a legality would make things a little funny first.

"You might have to get married again in order to secure the divorce."

Harsh and I looked at each other and then squarely at the lawyer. What on earth was he saying?

He pointed at the wedding pictures. Not one of them had my face showing; the veil was long and almost opaque.

"You do not have a marriage certificate, and the court will not accept the military order that was issued after your wedding. The new law for the mandatory civil marriage certificate came into effect right around the time the two of you got married. And these pictures absolutely will not work, so you do have to get married again for the backdated certificate and new pictures."

"No," I said before I could even form a thought.

"Ouch," Harsh muttered.

We looked at each other and burst into laughter.

I loved the way he made me laugh; I loved that we got each other's jokes; that we loved watching *Sex and the City* together; that we could dance together and get drunk together; and that he behaved himself at that time, at least, when he was drunk.

But seriously, no.

Why couldn't I have said no to him in the first place? We would have made very good friends in some world, if only we had stopped short of what we had tried to become instead, I lamented as the lawyer rubbed his temples.

Suddenly, Harsh nudged my arm with his elbow, and I followed his gaze to his phone—he was holding it under the table where he had typed, "Don't laugh—as it is, he thinks we aren't serious about the divorce."

I stifled a giggle, and the lawyer looked up, confused. I coughed and covered my mouth.

The screen lit up again. He had typed, "Wipe that smile off, cadet."

I completed the rest of that military academy threat for him on my phone's screen as he watched avidly, "Shove it up your ass, sir."

He laughed and typed, "Let's go get street food at that place we went to last time, before I drop you home."

I sank back in my chair.

Why did he enjoy the chase so much? He did not want to be a husband at all, and I had missed all the signals. But it was also too late to be friends now. No matter how much he genuinely wanted it.

The lawyer continued, "We really need a wedding card, at least, to get this mutual consent case filed."

I immediately produced the tattered copy of the wedding invitation that I had preserved and finally found in one of my old boxes. The lawyer now seemed satisfied and started making some calls.

When he was done, he put the wedding card right on top of the other papers in our black file and closed it, securing it with the red thread dangling on both sides.

"Take this to the paralegal," he said to the peon who had appeared at the door.

I watched as the evidence of our sacred union, preserved in one of the boxes that had traveled with me over 13 homes, was now taken away from me—there was no way I could have it back or stop its journey to a courthouse.

I decided to reply to the message he had typed for me to read a few minutes ago.

"Forget it—go crawl back into your hellhole and learn what it's like to not have a Mrs. Chauhan by your side, or rather, a Victim Chauhan, by your side."

He looked at the final message I typed on the screen and clenched his jaw.

Just as well, I decided, as I booked my own cab, to head home to my child.

As I was leaving, he slipped into the personality of the threatening ex once more. "What do you mean, victim? I will cut you off from the child if you talk like this."

I laughed and said, "You weren't going to put in any visitation if I hadn't asked for it on your behalf. So let's not go there. And let me ask you this—would you like your daughter to land up with a guy like you?"

He kept quiet, for a change.

"Let's co-parent her—it's the least she deserves. You may not have been the husband of anyone's dreams, but you can be the father she will always need. And don't worry about me—I can get street food on my own."

Six months passed. The divorce was granted easily; there was no court case. And we were only to show up for the court hearings—three in all over a period of six months. The only hiccup came when we were presented for the final hearing.

"Are you sure you have agreed to this? You have literally taken nothing after 10 years of marriage—how am I supposed to believe you can bring up your child with just this much? And what about you?" the judge looked down at me and demanded.

This middle-aged lady was clearly wise and well exposed to all that a Rajput last name could mean. She was asking me a not-so-veiled question - have you been forced or coerced into such an arrangement?

How could I explain to her that I only wanted my dignity and my sanity? That I had my daughter, my education, and a career and hence did not need his money—the very reason for the demise of our marriage, amongst other things? How could I tell her about the indignity of being trapped in the pages of a register that he asked his soldiers to maintain to record the price of every vegetable and fruit that I bought—which he duly produced in front of the senior officer and his wife, who questioned him on why he was asking me to leave?

After he had shown them the register that had logged every expense he had borne for me and the child, this aghast couple had asked me why I hadn't left earlier.

With the lawyer restlessly milling around, looking at his watch and many others in line behind us, I simply said, "I don't need anything. If I had my way, I wouldn't take even this much."

Harsh continued to look at his feet, and I wanted to ask him if his manhood was now as big as the Chauhan surname.

She was not convinced though and ordered me to present her with an affidavit stating what I had just said. The lawyer and my soon-to-be ex exchanged worried glances, and I saw immediate relief on their faces when I agreed.

"The divorce will be granted two weeks later instead of today," the lawyer informed us after we came outside into the corridor, "on the 12th of March."

"12th of March?" I said, as I almost choked.

"Yes, why?" he countered.

"Let it be," Harsh said in a low growl.

"It's his birthday," I answered, as I ignored the soon-to-be ex.

The lawyer did not say another word. He went back to the judge and came out a few moments later.

"March 11th—that's the new date for your final divorce hearing."

Two weeks later, as the divorce was granted, and we went home, I closed the door and wondered where to go.

Turns out I wouldn't be able to throw those doors open in a hurry.

We went into lockdown the very next day—our daughter's school announced that the school was officially closed.

My grief now had nowhere to hide.

I could not go out into the world and melt into the crowd of professionals doing their jobs, parents doing their parenting, friends doing their thing. I was here, alone and without distraction. I was face-to-face with my grief.

He landed up the very next day, cake in hand, ready to celebrate his birthday. I decided to leave the father and daughter alone, but he insisted

I stay. So I stayed and clicked their pictures, refusing with a laugh his constant pressure to have a piece of cake and feed him a piece too. The memory of him throwing a piece of cake on the floor as I tried to feed him on a previous birthday, because his parents were watching, was still too fresh. The memory of every arrow he had shot at me, including taking away the last name that he had forced me to take on—without even leaving room to accommodate the identity my parents had given me – was too fresh for me.

That night, before sleeping, my daughter asked me, "Mama, why did you look so sad today? Were you not happy that it was Papa's birthday?"

I kissed her hand and gently said, "I wish him a long life and will always be happy for him on this day. He is your father and that makes him very precious to me."

"Then were you sad because you both got divorced only yesterday?"

I smiled at her as my heart almost stopped, before I answered, "No, darling, the divorce happened between me and him, not us as parents. I am sad because I am not sure how not to be Mrs. Chauhan again. I feel like an outsider somehow."

"But you will always be a Chauhan, Mama – because you are Mama to a Chauhan."

Finally, without any conditions, someone had given me a name.

I was not Miss Mahapatra, the daughter who had let her parents down. I was not the ex Mrs. Chauhan. I would now forever be Mama Chauhan.

And so I took on my daughter's name.

Months later, during the pandemic, on one of his weekend stay overs at my place, he asked, as we both sat down for the customary movie and a drink after the child had slept, "I was going through your social-media pages and saw that you have now styled yourself as Devangini Mahapatra Chauhan—I had thought you would let the burdensome

Chauhan surname go as soon as you had a chance."

I smiled as I watched how far he had come—he did not berate me for posting a selfie any longer and did not call me a potentially loose character of a woman who was setting a terrible example and embarrassing her young nephews (on his side) by smiling so broadly that it looked provocative (only to him). He had noticed my name. I was visible to him. I was a separate entity.

Finally.

"Your name had been my honor, not a burden. Just like the one I inherited from my father. And this head can carry a crown with two diamonds. Yet you weren't so sure. Anyhow, I now go by my daughter's name—I am not a victim of yours any longer. I am still a Chauhan— just a different one."

He raised his glass and nodded his head in praise. "Spoken like a woman of substance," he said. "Don't let anyone take that away."

I smiled and drank to that.

And then he gently said, "And please tell my daughter that we are not bringing her up to simply get her married someday."

It's all he needed to say.

That day, I forgave the man who never apologized for the wounds he gave me.

Three years later, I get to hear different opinions about the choices I have made. Because apparently we may have gotten over the divorce—but my Indian relatives are not able to.

The same toxic family member who had told me I should be happy because I chose the divorce myself apparently now says, "You both are still clearly hung up on each other. I don't understand the *setting*." She emphasizes the term "setting" as if it is a dirty word that maligns us.

Oftentimes, in India, *setting* is a word used to depict an arrangement of convenience between two or more people. And that's what my effort to build a new family dynamic was being reduced to.

So here's my identity once and for all—this is not just some "setting," Indian Karen. This is my family. And in answer to the question you posed on the day my divorce was granted: we do not choose divorce. We choose ourselves. Because look at the little soul that's watching me for cues. How can I not model better choices? How can I not break generational curses?

And I am a proud Mama Chauhan who has made it possible with two lion-hearted men who expanded their spirits to accommodate this equation and show up fully.

Today, we are the proud parenting unit to the blessing of a child we have—me, him, and my soul's partner in crime. I have actually moved so far ahead that I am now able to look at Harsh like the father of my child, and nothing more. But even when we were married, I knew we would eventually be separated and divorced, so I think, after I stopped trying to hold on to the marriage stubbornly, I was able to move ahead even while I was married. And that's why I see him for the qualities he has as a son, a dad, and an army officer. I spent enough time with him observing just those parts without expecting him to be a husband. Maybe that's why I am able to accommodate him in our lives and our family.

For me, the main thing was: how we behave in our divorce will shape how our child sees herself as the product of a divorced couple. For the rest of her life. And the roar in my heart did not permit anyone to potentially malign or play with her identity or her sense of self.

So I stood up for myself—finally—so that I could do right by her. And today, no one who meets her is able to tell that she comes from a so-called broken home.

All because I stuck to my guns—all because I didn't blink.

Devangini Mahapatra Chauhan is an award-winning publisher who has been covered many times in the Indian media thanks to her efforts to contribute to the self-publishing landscape. Her publishing house **And All Publishing LLC** now has a presence in the U.S. and India. She is also the author of the bestselling book *The Aftermath of Ever After in 99 Poems*. Additionally, she also has a book-coaching practice based on mental wellness and excellence meta modeling philosophies such as psychometrics and neurolinguistic programming. She is a qualified practitioner in both fields. Her website **www.studioandall.com** as well as her Instagram (@devanginimahapatra) and LinkedIn (Devangini Mahapatra Chauhan) pages will tell you more!

It Ends With Me

JESSIE ARORA

Jessie baby,

I see you in so much pain. I see you looking around frantically for when you'll get the affection and love you're desperate for. I see you hurting yourself time and time again, not to hurt them, but to just be seen. Maybe the sight of blood will scare them and make them realize what they're doing. Maybe seeing you in such a dire state will wake them up. If they can't see the part of you that's lovable, maybe they'll see the part of you that hurts so deeply, surely they're not heartless.

Mom didn't even know you had taken the whole bottle of Tylenol that night. She could only feel the pressure of the mortgage on her shoulders. Dad didn't know you would take knives into the bathroom. He only knew the schedule of relentless bills that showed up constantly.

You didn't know this then, but know this: they fantasized about their own deaths too. Dad thought about it once in a while, but Mom tried a few times when things got really bad at home. They couldn't see your pain because they didn't know how to deal with their own, not to mention, stupid Bollywood taught them that suicide was the ultimate sacrifice. Maybe that's where you learned that, too. Your nose was always glued to the TV screen the minute a new Amitabh film came out on VHS.

They were not able to be the parents you needed then, I know, and for that I am deeply sorry. I know the memories will never disappear from your mind, but would you believe me if I told you that the pain you felt in those horrible moments would become your biggest superpower? Would you believe me if I told you that the love you were so desperate for is received in droves? Would you believe me if I told you that your parents become your biggest cheerleaders and your best friends? I know, it all sounds impossible from where you stand. But believe me, it happens.

It took a lot of time and hard work for you to change the thoughts, beliefs, and actions that were taught to you, but you did it. In fact, you changed so fearlessly that they changed too. Because you inspired them and showed them how to love in a different way. You'll be 43 when Dad tells you he's sorry and that he's proud of you, and Mom, well... Mom won't leave you alone now, because all she feels from you is the love, power, and courage that she also needed all those years that she felt alone. She feels so alive and joyful when she's around you. Don't tell Natasha or Irwin, but when you're 45 she tells you that you were always her favorite.

With this much love, Jessie baby, and with this much support, you will never seek love in the wrong places, at the hands of anyone who can't honor and care for the love you bring to this world. They love you more than anything, even if in the beginning it didn't feel like that. You won't want a love that is any less from anyone else ever again. Believe me. In the meantime, I'm sending you these angel wings so that when you need to, you can slip them on, in your dreams and come see how beautiful life is where I am now.

Endless love,

Jessie

July 14, 2021

It was a sunny Wednesday afternoon when I received a text message from my sister, Natasha. She was with her 5-year-old son, Rohin, at a community soccer practice in the neighborhood.

"Look who's here," she wrote while sending a picture of a little 4-year-old baby girl.

"Who is that?" I asked, as I didn't recognize her at all.

She then sent another picture of the baby girl's father coaching her during her soccer game.

My ex-husband.

The baby girl is light-skinned with curly brown hair. Without a doubt, I knew who the mother was. My body began to tremble. I fell to my kitchen floor, and I began to cry hysterically. The cool tiles touched my forehead, and I finally remembered to breathe. I tried to pick myself up off the floor, but my knees are weak. Ding, ding, ding, my phone continued to notify me of incoming messages. My sister continued to communicate with me in a one-sided conversation as I processed what I always knew. What was never validated, what was beaten out of me. The stolen opportunities, the unfair circumstances, the unnecessary violence—my body felt it all over again.

Eight years after leaving him, eight years of growth, therapy, rebuilding, and healing, my body remembered everything, and I couldn't control it. I let it take over. I let myself roll onto my side and clutch my belly. I let myself wail. I let myself grieve. An hour later, another notification dinged.

"Are you okay?" she asked.

"No," I responded.

"I'm sorry, I thought you would have already known," she assumed.

"No, I didn't," I replied. "I'll message you later, Natasha. I hope Rohin has a good game."

I left the conversation and entered into the hell of my memories.

I had cultivated a good life for myself. It took me eight years to finally get out of the debt I had gotten myself into when I was with him. I finally had a stable career of my own where I wasn't jumping from job to job, juggling his expectations and needs. I spent the last eight years focusing on me, who I want to be, and remembering who I was before I let him into my life. I tapped into my innate gifts to help others tap into theirs and support themselves. I had a flourishing holistic wellness business. I had a large community. I had rebuilt the relationships with most, if not all, of my family members. My relationship with my brother Irwin and my sister, Natasha, was the strongest they had ever been. I got to be the fun aunt and watch my nieces and nephews grow up. Even though I was single the whole time, I was never alone or lonely.

In fact, I appreciated my solitude as it gave me more time to know myself.

I remember the times when, despite being married, being around his two children, our clients, his family, and our mutual friends, I only ever felt alone.

We'd go to church every Sunday and I felt alone.

We'd go to his parent's house for Christmas and I'd feel alone.

His children would be over on the weekends and I'd feel alone.

We'd attend our friends' weddings and I'd feel alone.

Sometimes we'd be watching TV on the same couch and I'd still feel alone.

I felt especially alone when I would go to bed by myself. He said he was a night owl, and he had to wind down before he went to bed. Soon into the marriage, I realized he had multiple addictions that only the late-night hours could satisfy.

I abandoned myself so completely in that relationship that even though I felt the deep loneliness that I did, I was still okay with it, as long as he said he chose me, and he showed me that he chose me—even if what he said and did was violent. That violence was the only marker of love I knew. It was so deeply ingrained in me that it was okay, it was normal, and it was our unique love.

Those were the loneliest and darkest days of my life.

On paper, I had a partner. In our community, we looked good together. We made it look good on the outside, but on the inside, I had never known so much pain.

Throughout my marriage, I thought of my mother and father often. I understood why my mother never left my father. I understood the rage my father harbored and how torn he was. I understood the role their community played in my parents' toxic patterns and choices. I understood why our entire family loved and respected my parents so much. Of course they would, considering every dirty little secret was kept behind closed doors and nobody needed to know what was really going on.

I understood them because I had become them.

Come to think of it now, it makes sense how I went from their home to his. There were such similar patterns and behaviors. Such similar feelings of loneliness and estrangement even though we were all together and yet apart.

Six years into the marriage, 2009

Our house was a two bedroom semi-detached townhome. I was in the main bedroom. The walls were painted yellow. I had read somewhere that the color yellow helps cultivate joy and playfulness.

I had been bleeding profusely for three days, and it seemed to be getting worse. I was cramping terribly. At that moment, I had come out of the shower and wrapped myself in a big towel. My body felt weak; I needed to rest. I lay down on the bed.

I knew I was miscarrying. Again. No point in going to the hospital. I knew what this was. It'll pass. I began to cry. It started as a small, quiet release of emotions and grew into a louder cry. A cry of grief. A cry of not being good enough. A cry of being defective and damaged. A cry of being alone.

He heard me, I guess. He opened the door, and I could see he was annoyed that I was emotional once again. He asked me what was wrong, not because he cared, but because he didn't want to be a jerk. Fully in my pain, I reacted.

"What do you care?" I blurted out.

"What do I care? What do I care?" He repeated and asked condescendingly, threateningly.

He reached towards me and ripped the towel off my body, leaving me naked over the sheets. He had seen me naked hundreds of times, but this time he wasn't invited. Immediately, I shriveled into a ball as I covered my nakedness. "What do I care?" He kept repeating as he grabbed my arms and shook me, prying my body apart so that I would expose my bare body. He wanted me to feel weak, small, and pathetic. That gave him power. The towel was all I had, and he wanted it. Covering myself up was all I could do, and he wanted that too. When there was nothing left to take, he wanted more. I swung wildly so he would let go of me, but he didn't. He pulled at my legs and pulled me off the bed. I tumbled onto the floor, kicking and screaming. That's when he mounted me, punching me in the face and covering my mouth with his hands. I don't remember what happened next.

My only vague memory thereafter is that he got up off me and kicked me in the stomach while I curled up into a ball on my side. He spat on me and walked away, and didn't even close the door behind him. He didn't even look back. He didn't even see the pool of blood beneath me, or at least that's what I like to believe. If I can convince myself that he didn't know, he didn't see, he didn't understand, then I can stay. I can keep trying. Maybe *I am* a bad communicator; maybe *I am* too emotional; maybe *I am* the jealous type; maybe *I am* not understanding how this works. My body is defective, so maybe my mind is too.

I wasn't dead yet, so it only made sense to keep trying.

Eight years into the marriage, 2011

William Osler Hospital, Brampton, Ontario. I had woken up on a stretcher, and I couldn't move my body. There were people hurrying and scurrying all around me. I was not in a room, but also, I was not in a hallway. I could hear other people all around me. Violent coughing, crying, and moaning. But I couldn't see anyone. Beeping of machines, footsteps, lots of bustling, hurrying footsteps. Rubber soles against vinyl floors, squeaky. I was wearing a yellow hospital gown. I was cold. They must have undressed me. I couldn't move my neck. There was some sort of contraption on it. Dammit! It didn't work. The bungee cord must have snapped, or maybe there wasn't enough distance between the mezzanine and the ground floor. Had I broken my neck?

For God's sake! I knew exactly what was coming next. This wasn't my first rodeo. This will be the fourth time they kept me with a Form 1 (which means the hospital could keep me involuntarily to undergo a psychiatric assessment, this would determine if I needed to be admitted for further care in a psych care facility. That process usually took three days).

Now I would have to answer a million questions to people who knew nothing about me and already labeled me crazy.

They don't care about me, they're just doing their job. I know how this goes. Just surrender, Jess, just be as pleasant as possible; otherwise, they're never going to let you go. Remember last time? Don't give them any trouble, and maybe this time you won't have to take the meds. Just be pleasant. There is no point in fighting this.

A nurse approached me. She was wearing periwinkle scrubs and white sneakers. I noticed a pretty, thin gold chain around her neck with a tiny letter A dangling from it. She had a clipboard and pen in her hand.

"Jessie Arora?" she asked.

"Yes," I responded automatically. But when I opened my mouth to speak, I could barely make a sound. It was less than a scratchy whisper. I must have messed up my neck in the jump.

Damn bungee cord!

"Do you know why you're here?" she asked.

I didn't say a thing. I just stared at my feet.

"Can you tell us what happened?" She continued to probe.

"I can't remember," I whispered, as my eyes welled up with tears and my chin quivered with fear.

"The police are here. They have some questions for you," she let me know.

Shit, I forgot about those guys. I had no intention of dealing with any of them this time around. I was so sure it would have worked. Okay, so now I needed to know who found me and what happened after that because I can't just tell the cops everything.

But why not? A voice whispered in my head. Why not just tell them like it is? You gotta stay for three days anyhow, and you can't change that. So just tell them everything and be as honest as possible, the voice in my head continued. All the while, my eyes darted back and forth from my feet to the nurse as she waited for a response.

"Okay," I whispered.

For the next three days, I was as cooperative and honest as I could be. More than ever before. They were able to remove the neck brace, but I still couldn't move my neck much at all. Luckily there weren't any broken bones, although I still wished the attempt at hanging myself in my gym had worked.

I told them everything.

The 10 years of endless cheating, the abuse, the broken bones, the fight that led up to this moment, the miscarriages, the financial burden, the constant unyielding suffering—and for the first time in my life, I felt heard. I didn't want to press charges, so there was no longer any need for the police. They matched me up with a South Asian psychologist who saw me twice a day. When I wasn't with her, I was sleeping in my room. Once, I decided to walk over to the TV room to disconnect just for an hour. I sat down on the couch, turned on the TV, and immediately I heard my name being called over the PA system. After telling them so much and revealing all my truth, I could have sworn they were calling me to meet with my psychologist, and she was going to tell me I'd need to stay for another seven days before I could be released.

Instead, when I got to my room, I saw my best friend, Jasvir, sitting on my bed. There was a plastic bag of clothing on the chair in the corner of the room, and a cup of Tim Hortons Earl Grey steeped tea, milky with the teabag still in, cupped between her hands.

My heart felt good seeing her; she knew all the things that made me feel good, but for some automatic, defensive reason, I was cold towards her, as if any of this was her fault.

"Who let you in? I told them I didn't want visitors," I said.

"I told them I was your sister," she responded.

Although she didn't know every single detail about the last ten years, she knew enough, and in that knowing, she never once told me to leave. She only ever supported me, even though I knew she knew it was never going to work. We never ever admitted to each other that it had to come to an end. Maybe that's why I was so cold towards her, because I didn't want her to be right. We talked, she held me. I cried. We both knew it was time.

In the span of those three days, I had finally been able to surrender to my ego and recognize that I had created this hell.

Yes, he was a big part of it, but why did I let it get this far? Why did I endure it year after year, beating after beating, lie after lie?

In the middle of the night on day three, I woke up in my sleep. It finally dawned on me.

I had become my parents.

It took me nine years to finally understand that I let it get this far because I was never being real. I was never really me. I was never letting myself be seen in my emotions or my struggles, and I definitely wasn't letting anybody in to help me. How could I possibly help myself if I couldn't get other perspectives, care, and compassion?

That's exactly how my parents did it for all those years. Push through, survive, everything is fine, don't tell anybody about what goes on in the house, and definitely don't talk about our emotions or challenges. It's like they grew up to believe that emotions were the bad guy—a bad word. Anger and violence were fully accepted and normalized, but talking about emotions… Oh no, no, we don't do that. What good would it do anyway? Crying, complaining, surrendering, and quitting gets us nowhere, so it's best we armor up, pretend to be fine, and do what's expected of us. The only other alternative is to be ostracized by society and to struggle even harder, alone.

I was already alone, though. So what difference did it make? I was already ousted by my family and friends. So what difference did it make? And I was already struggling and suffering at the hands of another human. So wouldn't it just make sense to struggle on my own, without his influence and control?

These thoughts were like a flashlight in my mind, shining concentrated beams on tiny moments where I found myself questioning myself. At the time, it felt like a warehouse full of thoughts in my head had been illuminated. But the truth was, I still needed more time. It was too much to process all at once. I went back to bed at 4 a.m. and by 8 a.m., I called him to pick me up so that I could be discharged and go home.

The phone rang three times, and I thought he'd still be sleeping. I was calling the gym, which for the time being was also our apartment.

He's not a morning person; how could he be with all that philandering in the late hours of the night? I'll call back in an hour, I thought.

On the fourth ring, a woman picked up. A voice I knew all too well. A voice that elicited such a visceral reaction in my body that it felt like my blood boiled in my veins and my skin crawled with insects. A feeling I was so familiar with, but never did anything about it.

It was the woman he had been with multiple times over a long period of time, maybe the whole eight years.

They both denied it over and over again, making me feel like I was batshit crazy. I would approach him, and be gaslighted. I would accuse him and be beaten black and blue. I would behave badly towards her, and be painted as a monster.

But on this particular day, I felt absolutely nothing. In fact, I wasn't surprised at all. I knew what he would say in his defense if I even brought it up. I was stressed; I couldn't handle the gym on my own. Everybody was asking about you. I couldn't concentrate. I needed help, so I just asked her to come sit at the reception desk for the day. She's just answering the phone; what's the big deal? I heard it all in my head, and at that time, it even made sense. "Please ask him to pick me up from the hospital now; I'm being released," I said to her. "Oh, of course, right away, Jessie," she responded with such care and compassion. I worked two jobs and managed the gym for years, and he couldn't manage *three days?* I was gone for *three days* and was already replaced, and I wasn't surprised at all. If I was anything, I was numb.

Thirty minutes later, I was sitting in the car with him on my way home. Neither of us mentioned her name, what she was doing there, or why.

"Are you okay?" He asked.

"Yes, I'm just tired, and I want to sleep," I responded, my favorite way of avoiding life.

On the way home, I looked out the window the entire time and didn't say a word.

We passed my parents' street to their restaurant. I saw their car in the parking lot. They must have just gotten there. They usually started prepping for customers 30 minutes before they opened their doors.

Dad must have turned on the gas burners. I could smell the fumes of the first flame catching the pilot. I could smell the first pot of *Kadak Chai* on the stove by now. Would it boil over into the burner the way it had hundreds of times before? Mom was probably counting the bills and coins in the cash register. The employees would be filling up the jugs of water and the napkin dispensers. One of them would be sweeping the front while another one was rushing around in the back to get the daily meals started. I could replay it all in my mind's eye the same way I had seen it for nearly 15 years before I left.

Before I chose him. Before I lost my parents.

What if I asked him to take me to my parents' restaurant instead? Deep down, I wanted to tell my mom everything and just cry in her arms, like

I did in Jasvir's arms the night before in the hospital. What if I chose a different path today? It was clear and right in front of me. Turn left to go back to Mom and Dad's, or go straight home with him.

Go straight.

Dad said he never wanted to talk to me ever again.

Go straight; at least I know what to expect there.

Go straight. I need to go back to sleep.

The best way I knew how to avoid my problems.

Sleep.

Just a little longer.

Just a little more, until I have no choice, and I'm forced to wake up, forced to make a change.

If only my life was as peaceful as my slumber.

I knew I had to make a change; I just didn't know how yet.

Nine years into the marriage, 2012

After three broken bones, three miscarriages, nine years of parental estrangement, bankruptcy, losing job after job, two failed businesses, and not an ounce of dignity within me, the only friend I still had, Jasvir, practically pulled me by my shirt collar, put me in her car, and told me I was leaving. No bags of clothing, no housewares, no memorabilia, no goodbyes.

He was at work; the kids were with their mothers. I hadn't packed anything in advance, so he had no idea. I did, however, cut my dreadlocks two nights before and neatly placed them in a photo box.

To this day, I'm convinced he knew it was over in that very moment when I walked out of my bedroom without my crown. To grow dreadlocks in observance of the Rastafarian way was to wear a royal crown and never ever cut it. I had become a Rastafarian for him. I had converted to Christianity for him. I left my God to believe in His—all to convince him of how worthy I was.

I was left with something between a choppy crew cut and a messy butch. I looked like a stray cat that had just come out of a street brawl. He looked at me in disgust, turned around and walked toward the couch, where he had been sleeping for the past year.

That night I couldn't sleep. I woke up at 3 a.m., needing to use the bathroom. I opened up my bedroom door and as I was about to walk out of the bedroom he was laying there on the floor, sleeping against my door, with a butcher knife in his hands. I froze in my tracks. I tried to play it calm and cool. Stepped over him and asked him what in God's name he was doing, as though seeing him in this way didn't bother me at all.

You don't scare me, I thought.

You have no idea what I've seen or been through at my parents' house.

What is this child's play?

Do something if you're going to do something!

My mind was running a marathon of wild thoughts. I went to the bathroom and splashed water on my face.

Am I seeing things? Is this for real? What the hell is he thinking? Is this how it ends?

I took one deep breath in, dropped my shoulders, puffed up my chest with my proverbial armor, and readied my body for a fight. I came back out of the bathroom, ready for a beating and maybe my death.

He was gone.

I turned and looked beyond the hallway, where he was now sitting on the black leather couch, with the butcher knife now on the glass coffee table in front of him.

Slowly, I closed the door to my bedroom, crawled back in bed, and texted Jasvir, "Hi, I know it's late. Text me in the morning, please. I'm afraid," as my hands shook violently, and my heart was pounding in my throat.

It was time. No more sleeping through it.

I had been living with Jasvir for three weeks now.

The so-called husband and I would go back and forth via text, arguing, fighting, insulting each other. I finally got him to agree to hand over some of my belongings to Jasvir. That night she brought home three black garbage bags with most of my clothing, laden with broken shards of glass from the picture frames on the walls he had punched when he went home and realized I was gone. I threw everything away.

I started from scratch, quite literally.

No pictures, no books, no laptop, no documents, no clothing, no jewelry, no job, no money, nothing.

Absolutely nothing.

I was so afraid I didn't even trust the police to protect me. It was better to just walk away and not fight for anything. By that time, I had already lost anything and everything that was actually important to me. So the material things didn't matter much at all anymore. When there is absolutely no dignity left, there is nothing left to fight for.

I was sleeping in one of Jasvir's kid's bedrooms because they had just moved away to university. A small twin mattress on the floor and a desk completed the room. For the next three months I don't remember anything other than sleeping a lot, like, *a lot* a lot. I didn't go to work, I didn't cook, I didn't clean, I didn't contribute to the house in any positive way. I know my friend was worried about me. I could see it in the way she looked at me. She could only play mommy to me for so long. What didn't she do for me? She lent me her car if I wanted to go out. She gave me a job, she sat with me for hours and talked to me, she let me cry all day if I needed to. She even registered me in local self-help and spirituality courses, something I was into before my marriage.

Just as my mom had seen and accepted the spiritual part of me by enrolling me into my first Reiki, tarot and palm reading classes when I was 18 years old, Jasvir was leading me back to my spiritual self too. Back to a version of myself that was more in tune with my own intuition and self-awareness. A version of myself that I left behind when I met him.

Everything stopped because I started to believe in everything he believed because he said so. Just like Mom and Dad used to respond "because we said so," to anything I would question or push against.

"Can I sleepover at Naniji's on the weekend?" I'd ask.

"No," one of them would respond without even a second thought.

"Why not?" I'd ask.

"Because we said so."

"Can I go to the movies with my friends after school?" I'd ask.

"No," with a blank stare on their faces.

"Why not?" I'd ask.

"Because we said so."

"Can I go on that school trip to Montreal with the rest of the class?" asking with excitement, surely they'd see the importance this trip had for me.

"No," without any consideration.

"Why not?" I still asked, even though I probably already knew the answer.

"Because we said so."

And so it went until I became 16 and stopped asking.

Finally, after years in my father's house and then years with my husband, I began to see the patterns, the similarities, the limited self-awareness, agency, self-worth, and autonomy.

Who am I?

I'm 34 years old.

How could I possibly not know who I am? By 35, Jasvir had three kids, a house, a marriage, and her own successful business. By 35, my mom had three kids, a marriage and a successful business.

What have I done? Not only do I not have anything to show for the past 34 years, but I have also lost all sense of who I am. It took me three months away from him to see that I had only repeated everything that both my mother and father had done to each other for all those years.

Our circumstances were different, but the patterns, beliefs, and behaviors were the same. It took the last hospital visit for me to be heard by someone. It took a life-threatening scare for my friend to finally see me. It took my own deep inner reflection through despair and depression to finally understand that I had never understood self-worth, value, or even love. Never. I was never taught; how could I possibly understand?

It only made sense that I recreated an environment that felt familiar, and if *I* created a familiar environment for myself, then is it possible that's what my parents did in their marriage too? Is this why they could never understand my emotions? Because they weren't taught to understand them either? Because they were taught to avoid them, to bury them, to react and project in violent ways, so we never had a chance to see the small hurting children still inside each of us?

There was no need for emotions when all we had to do was survive, but how long would this survival contest continue? Did I need to be in survival mode? Were Mom and Dad still in survival mode? Were they still fighting at home? Who else was in this competition of optics and appearances? Nobody would know unless one of us finally opened up. But sadly, I knew it was never going to be them.

It had to be me.

The chance to be a parent was taken away from me three times, and all I needed at that time were my parents. I needed them to stand beside me, but there was no way they'd stand beside me if I wasn't willing to stand beside them. I had to really open up my eyes and see them as humans on their own personal journey before I could see them as parents.

I had to truly see them in order for them to truly see me.

It was time for me to open up my eyes and open up my heart.

Three months after I left my marriage

I drove to the parking lot of my parents' restaurant. Just sitting there in the driver's seat of Jasvir's car, staring at the food decals plastered on the front windows. Channa Bhatura $4.99, Thali $8.99, and Mango Lassi $3.99. Between the images of the food and sweets, I could see heads bobbing about in the shop. Customers ordering, employees serving, but I didn't see Mom or Dad. Maybe they weren't there. Maybe they had stepped out to run errands. If they weren't there, at least I had tried—

right? The universe isn't aligning, so what else is there for me to do? I was looking for escape routes already, and I hadn't even gone inside yet. I saw the door open and customers came outside. Nobody I recognized . I took a deep breath in, dropped my shoulders, slipped on my proverbial armor, and prepared my body for a stressful and what I thought would be an inevitably disappointing encounter.

As I walked into the restaurant, I noticed the shelving units had changed. They were no longer a deep marbled blue, but instead they were a rich cherrywood. The direction of the food showcases had changed, and one of the older units was gone entirely. The self-serve savory dispensers were no longer in the far right corner. Now there was a TV mounted on the wall. There was much more seating to accommodate more customers. Plants hung from the ceiling, giving the restaurant a much warmer vibe. I recognized the employee at the front counter, and we warmly smiled at each other.

"Sat Sri Akal," I greeted her, and she greeted me in return. I made my way to the dividing screen that blocked customers' view from the door leading into the back kitchen.

I walked towards the office. Mom was sitting down, eating her lunch. That in itself was a sight I had never seen before. In the past, she always ate standing up while she continued to work with one hand, or direct and delegate tasks to the employees. To see her in silence in the office, eating peacefully, was a foreign sight. Automatically, I assumed they had fought, and she had distanced herself for a short while.

"Hi, Mom," I said, as she looked up at me.

I didn't even give her an opportunity to respond before I rolled up an office chair and sat right in front of her.

"You okay?" I asked.

"Yeah, fine," she responded as a single tear began to roll down her cheek, and she simultaneously put another piece of roti in her mouth.

"I need to speak to you and Dad," I told her.

"What happened?" She automatically responded, as though there was more bad news. "What now?"

"It's nothing bad, I just want to speak to the two of you together," I said.

She finished eating minutes later and went into the kitchen to get Dad.

I got up from the seat and stood in the narrow hallway as the two of them sat at the desk.

Dad and I didn't greet each other. He simply cleared his throat, pursed his lips tight, sat down and looked at my face. Without even a second thought, my face was in my hands. My fingers pushing against my eyes, trying to make sense of all the things I wanted to say in my mind.

"Just say it," he said, his voice gruff with emotion.

My therapist, my spiritual teachers, my friend, all their faces flashed in front of my eyes, and all I could hear in my mind was all the things they told me to say to him.

Instead, all that came out was this.

"I know I've hurt you a lot over the last ten years. I'm sorry. I made a lot of choices that weren't good for me or good for the family. I'm sorry. I don't know what I was thinking. I'm sorry. I left him. I've been living with Jasvir for three months now. It's over."

I started to feel dizzy, but instead of sitting on a chair, I sat on the floor directly in front of him, looking up into his eyes, like a little girl once again.

I found myself lowering my forehead to touch his feet, and all that came out of my mouth was a stream of, "Please forgive me, please forgive me, please forgive me, please forgive me."

Tears were pouring down my face, my mother was sobbing, and my father was crying too but really holding back as he sniffled again and again to try and keep it all in.

He put his hand on my head and said, "It's okay, *beta*, it's okay. We're here for you. We were always here for you."

He got up and peeled me off the floor and took me into his arms.

Mom ran away into the kitchen. Probably to tell the employees what was happening. She was clearly overjoyed. She couldn't cry too much; otherwise it would be too hard for her to reel it back in. I could tell she wanted to give me and Dad some space.

I hugged him for a long while and he let me. The thoughts of my therapist came into my head again: tell him how he hurt you too and how in fact he wasn't there for you. Tell him that his behavior all those years wasn't okay, tell him that this doesn't mean everything's hunky-dory and that we really need to sit down and talk more.

Tell him! My inner voice screamed at me. *No,* I reasoned with myself. *Not now, not today. Just let this be what it is.* He said he had to go back to work as he dried his eyes and patted me on the shoulder.

"Okay," I said. "Thank you," I awkwardly blurted out, sounding childlike and foolish in a purely vulnerable moment when words would not do justice.

Mom came back into the office to be with me. We both sat at the desk. She looked into my eyes and said everything was going to be okay. We both exhaled together.

"I had another miscarriage last month," I informed her.

"Good," she responded immediately. "It's better that way, move on now," she continued without any hesitation, and also without any compassion.

I sighed again.

Even though I knew she was right, it hurt like hell. She was the epitome of tough love, and in that very moment I understood her a little more. I felt her pain, and I couldn't help but know that moving forward, I had to soften. The circumstances I grew up in created a hard exterior, one that I prided myself for, only to realize that in actuality it was *their* pain that I was carrying. She didn't have the choice to soften. I do, and it begins now.

April 25, 2024

Akaasha, Meharvan, Zorawer,

Not a day goes by when I don't think of you in some way or another. When I see baby birds with their mothers, I think of you. When I see my friends having children, I think of you. When I look at my belly in the mirror after I shower, I think of you. When I am with my nieces and nephews, I think of you. You have been with me. I have never not been your mommy, and you have never not been my babies.

I want you to know that although I desperately wanted you, begged God for you, I would not have been able to be the mommy you needed me to be. I needed more time to learn, to understand, to change. I needed more time to undo the pain and the hurt that flowed through our families' veins. I needed more time to become the love I was always looking for.

I know if you could see me now, you'd be proud of me.

Akaasha, I'd teach you about your creative power and help you cultivate confidence in your self-expression. I'd be a good example of how to speak your truth and not be shameful or guilty. I'd show you how interconnected you are with the Sun and the Moon, with you in the middle, the bridge to miracles and magic. Anything your brothers can do, you could do too.

In fact, don't tell them, but you can do even more, not because you're different or better for being a girl, but because you hold the power to quite literally change the world.

Meharvan and Zorawer, I'd help you find good examples of a King, a Warrior, a Magician, and a Lover so that you can understand how you could be all of them whenever you needed. I'd listen to your stories and help you be whoever you wanted to be. I'd help you cultivate your connection to your purpose and your passion. I'd teach you how to understand your emotions so that they become the fuel for your creativity.

Above all, Mere Pyare, I would make space for joy, play, and pleasure in my life so that you could see what it means to truly live, not by the expectations of society, but by the birthrights and gifts of life bestowed upon us from the creator. We'd sing and dance every chance we got. We'd celebrate our uniqueness and revel in the beauty of our differences. Together, we would create a sanctuary of love and acceptance where you could blossom into the incredible beings you were meant to be.

I imagine the laughter that would fill our home, the adventures we would embark on, and the lessons we would learn from each other every single day. You would be my greatest teachers, guiding me to be the best version of myself so that I could guide you through the journey of life with wisdom and grace.

Even though you are not physically here with me, your presence lingers in my heart and soul, shaping me into the person I am today. I carry you with me always, a reminder of the love that could have been and the love that still exists in the depths of my being.

As I write these words, tears of both sorrow and gratitude flow from my eyes. Sorrow for the moments we will never share, but gratitude for the profound impact you have had on my life. You have taught me what it means to love unconditionally, to cherish every moment, and to never take anything for granted.

My dear Akaasha, Meharvan, and Zorawer, wherever you may be, know that you are loved beyond measure. You are my greatest blessings, and I will carry you with me always, until the end of time.

With all my love,

Your mommy

Jessie Arora is a distinguished psychosomatic therapist based in Toronto, Canada, with a profound commitment to holistic health and empowerment. With nearly 20 years of experience in the industry, she specializes in addressing complex issues through integrative approaches that include Cognitive Behavioral Therapy (CBT), Neuro-Linguistic Programming (NLP), Shamanic Studies, Spinal Energetics, Reiki, Somatic Therapy, and Art Therapy.

Being born to first-generation immigrants from Punjab, India, and being brought up in the multicultural and western society of Canada in the 1970s, she brings a deep understanding of cultural nuances and psychological dynamics to the discourse.

Beyond her therapeutic practice, Jessie has facilitated wellness retreats globally, spanning continents such as Africa, Indonesia, South America, and North America. These experiences have enriched her understanding of global wellness practices and cultural diversity.

With a focus on embodiment and empowerment, Jessie continues to inspire and empower individuals to achieve holistic well-being and personal transformation.

The Way Back Home to Me

MATINA SINGH

I was sitting in my living room, in complete darkness, listening to the silence. My children were sleeping peacefully in the room upstairs. Even though I was sitting in silence, there was a tornado in my mind, going from one end to the other, threatening to destroy my self-confidence.

This silence that I had so yearned for, now here, seemed daunting. Why was I not able to fully enjoy it? What else had I wanted from life? The safe and loving environment that I created in the last one and a half years with my children—was it enough? Enough to make this "broken" family feel whole again?

There were so many questions inside of me, but no one to answer them. Honestly, I was doubting if I had even made the right decision to end my marriage. I started telling myself that it wasn't so bad and that perhaps if I had stayed, we wouldn't be a broken family!

"Broken family" was a label that I had received from society. And you know what was worse? I had taken it on as if I had no other choice. So many of our life choices come from the environment and society we grow up in.

And I felt that I had failed them all, but most of all, I had failed myself.

One thing that I quickly understood was that under the umbrella of culture and society, so many of us are limited in our life experiences! We are told who to be, how to be, what is accepted, and what is "wrong."

Now, looking back at that Matina who sat in her living room doubting herself, to where I am today, with the choices that I made in life, and the worth that I see in the mirror, it is a shift that I couldn't have imagined.

Before I can share the journey from doubt to self-love and self reflection, I need to take you back to the parts of my life that shaped my marriage, my marriage itself and the journey after!

At the age of seven, we moved from India to the Netherlands, where I grew up. My parents chose a small town to raise us in because they believed it would provide a better handle on raising good, cultured girls that would get married off into Sikh families, because that was their sole task as parents,at least, that's how they saw it.

Their checklist for us looked like this:

- Get a good education
- Help them out at home and business
- Get a good job
- Marry a cultured Sikh guy from a well-off family, so that we wouldn't face any financial hardships

Nowhere in this list does it ask, "What does Matina want?" or, "What is Matina capable of?"

I love my parents and also understand that the circumstances they grew up in made them believe this checklist to be true. However, as a young adult, I began to question their decisions constantly, but I didn't have the guts to ever go against them. Instead, I learned to keep my feelings to myself.

As I had learned to keep pushing my feelings down and ignore them, the only checklist that I had for myself was for the *guy to like me!* Not for me to like him. Not for me to be in love with him. Just for him to like me, to want me, to pick me. This way of thinking was so normal for most of my upbringing, but now, looking back, I see how misplaced this was. It was crazy!

Never did I ask myself what *I wanted* because it was more important to fulfill my duty as the daughter in an Indian family.

When it came time for my marriage, my dad thought he needed to go to India to find me a suitable husband. Since my cousin's wedding was approaching, he decided to attend. There, he started noticing that the India he once knew did not exist anymore. The values, culture, and traditions that he had left behind in India that he was lovingly teaching his own family, were being readily abandoned. The culture was evolving. He was shocked by how much things had changed. This was not what he wanted for his daughters.

Once back, he had given up on the requirement that the boy needed to be from India. He decided to start in the Netherlands and the surrounding area to see if he could find me a good match.

I wondered what he had seen in India that made him rethink the *only way* I knew I was going to experience an arranged marriage. He didn't share much about it, only that first we will look locally verses looking abroad. "But how?" I wondered.

Apparently, Shaadi.com was the solution to it all! My sister was tasked to create my profile and start looking. I had so many questions but dismissed them all because I convinced myself that my parents knew what is best for me. After all, they arranged my sister's marriage and that had worked. Two matches emerged and the conversation between my parents and them began.

One match was in the Netherlands. "Let's see how things work out with the one here," my dad said.

I was curious and wanted to know more about this guy before the meeting. So, I convinced my sister to share more information.

I remember the day we were to meet, I had a job interview right before. I was supposed to meet him at the *Gurdwara* with my whole family. My mind should have been focused on the interview that was about to take place, but all I could think about is what this guy would be like.

What will he think of me?

Do I look okay?

I can't believe that I am about to meet the person who I possibly will marry!

I tried to shake it off to focus on the interview. The manager came in, and with my sweaty, clammy hands, I shook his hand. I came out of the interview not knowing how it went because I was so nervous.

My real interview happened later, when we stepped into the *Gurdwara* with my family. He was there with his cousin. We sat in one room, all of us together, and then we had an opportunity to meet separately in the main room in *Gurdwara*. I was so nervous that I didn't know what to say, so I laughed! That was my protection mechanism—laughter.

We spoke for about 10 to 15 minutes that day.

That was supposed to be enough to decide if we wanted to marry each other.

Things were progressing so quickly. After meeting him twice and after many chats on MSN, my Dad asked me what I thought of him. For the first time, I was asked what I wanted! Even though I was 25 at that time, I was a rookie when it came to relationships. I felt so lucky and thought I had fallen in love, so I told my dad, "Yes! He is the one!" Why? Because *he liked me* and was showing interest in *me!* The girl who wasn't allowed to be noticed, to be seen by others, was now being seen by her husband-to-be.

I truly thought I was doing right by my parents and myself. I realize now that while my only requirement was to be liked, I couldn't build a future on it. I even dismissed my mom's concern of alcohol consumption in his community. A stereotype I had heard but didn't understand. *How bad could it be?* I thought, *even Dad drinks once a while. This isn't an issue,* I reassured her. And myself.

After all, I was doing what was expected of me since I was a young girl.

Nobody told me to take a deep dive *within*. Never did I think about the type of partner I wanted, the life I would like to build with him and how we both would be with each other.

Questioning my life simply wasn't a part of my reality. It was always about following along, and doing the best that I could. At the beginning of my marriage, he drank on the weekends. It was his way to relax and enjoy himself. This is how the world speaks about alcohol, too. *Not a problem, I thought.*

A few years later, the drinking began on a daily basis. Every evening, he would stay downstairs, watching TV, and drinking, while I was in bed alone.

One night, I couldn't sleep and kept looking at the ceiling in the dark, wondering, Why aren't we speaking anymore? Why does he drink every night? Was my mom's concern right? Once again, I had so many questions but no answers.

I gathered some courage and went downstairs. Standing at the living room door, I peeked through and asked, "Are you coming to bed?"

Annoyed, he looked up and snapped, "Yes, later, you go to sleep."

With a sigh, I walked into the living room. There he was, once again—TV on, having his whiskey and busy on his phone. I sat down next to him.

"Please come up now, it is late, you need your rest too, and drinking every evening isn't good for you."

He looked at me with a straight face and said, "I am not doing anything wrong, I am sitting in my home enjoying a drink. You know the stress that I am under. I need this to relax."

Saddened, I looked at him, and I thought to myself, *the stress that you are under? What about me? I am working two jobs and doing everything I can to make this work but with little to no appreciation.* Yet, instead of voicing these thoughts, I kept quiet and walked back upstairs to our bedroom.

That night, I thought back to all the moments we spent and how the needs of others overpowered our own lives.

I laughed at myself, thinking that my life was my own. It never felt like mine to begin with. He felt responsible for supporting others and as a good wife, I took his responsibility as mine. As a result, we both worked and did what we could. If not supporting his family, then there were extended family members or friends who requested financial support. We kept supporting them. Why? Because he felt he needed to.

"We will figure this out," he always said, and I followed along.

I caught myself questioning his behavior more and more, and anytime I would voice it, we would end up in a heated argument. It seemed like a better idea to just play along and do what I could. My hard-earned money was never mine. His behavior left me feeling disheartened and sad inside. Still, I was showing up with a big smile and a there-is-nothing-wrong approach. I kept going.

Why was I so dismissive of my own feelings? Why didn't I learn better money management strategies growing up? What could I do to improve my financial situation? These were all questions that would come up, and I would push them away.

It wasn't until I got pregnant with my twin boys that things internally shifted for me. Now, it was all about my boys and the life I desired to give them.

The new mother in Matina was born as I gave birth!

The one who would say no—a simple word to say, right?

Not for me, not for the first five years of our marriage.

Any outsider would look at us and say, "They have their lives under control, a home, two cars, their own business - everything is going well for them."

Inside, there were so many imbalances—an imbalance in money, an imbalance in our relationship, and an imbalance in the values that we both held.

The simple word "NO" drastically changed my relationship. I no longer accepted his drinking each night. I didn't accept giving and sending money without having a plan for how we would repay it. I even told him that he couldn't help his friends and extended family until we actually had the money to give.

Reasonable?

Not to him.

Our arguments became ever-increasing. The disconnect spiraled even before I was ready to deliver the twins.

The joy of motherhood was tainted with my inner dissatisfaction. Going from a family of two to a family of four was a big shift for me. I hadn't adjusted to this big change yet, when we were faced with another big decision.

Our permanent resident application to Canada was approved. Would we move? After many conversations, we decided to take the plunge. My dear friend who visited asked me, "Why are you moving?" I looked at her and with a sigh I said, "This is my last attempt to save my marriage. I don't know what else I can do!" My inner thoughts were aired for the first time and it shook me even more to hear them erupt from inside me.

We took a year to make the shift happen and started our lives in a new country. As my boys were a year old now, I was ready to embrace work again. I found a position in marketing but didn't feel it was the right fit as I worked over 10 hours and brought work home daily. Just a few months in, I quit.

He didn't understand. He was more worried about what he would tell his family when I quit my job. I can still picture him, sitting on the brown leather sofa, looking at me with disbelief. As I sat on the far end of the other sofa, our eyes were spitting fire! None of us felt heard or understood—we both were in our heads with the stories we were telling ourselves.

He went on to say, "Why?" His logic: the kids are being taken care of by their grandparents, so there wasn't a need for me to want to care for my boys. The need was for me to make money.

I couldn't believe my ears! Had I heard him right? There wasn't a need for their own mother to take care of them? I was furious. Our toxic way of proving each other wrong continued. I quickly recognized that my value was in providing money versus being a wife or a mother.

A hard pill to swallow.

Crying at night and wondering how I had let this come this far became my norm. Our unwillingness to really listen and try to understand each other caused emotional abuse and turmoil, the drinking wasn't making it any easier. To me, it felt like I was alone in advocating for our relationship and our children.

Yet, I also dismissed my own feelings in hopes of keeping the peace at home.

After reviewing various jobs, I decided to take on a year-long course that would help me get a government job, earn more money, and help secure us financially. Maybe doing that would solve our finances, and in turn, our marriage.

A few months in, I had to take my boys for their annual check up.

"Mrs. Singh, how are you today?" the doctor said as he walked in with a smile.

I looked up and greeted him back.

Once we had gone over the regular checkup, he asked, "Do you have any questions or concerns?"

With hesitation, I asked, "Well, they are over two now and still don't speak much."

First, he put me at ease and said, "This is common with twins, as they have their own language that they embrace with each other. But tell me, how much do they interact with other children?"

"They don't, actually!" I quickly answered. "They are home all the time and are either watching TV or playing with each other."

He smiled and said, "Try having them interact with other kids."

My head went into overdrive. How will I do this? A daycare would help them along, being with other kids and getting a little more independence. The drive home, all I kept thinking about was how will I tell him? I did not recognize that this too was a red flag. Not being able to talk about life's big and small decisions without the fear of a fight was a battle—and not a marriage at all.

At first, I tried attending free events where other children would be present. But my boys weren't interested in the other kids. I knew the solution was daycare. A place they would go to everyday and learn how to socialize and interact. It truly seemed like the only way. But how would he react when I tell him?

At home, I shared with him that it was time to put the kids in daycare so they could open up and communicate more. Annoyed, he looked at me and said, "We have no money for daycare—you don't work yet!"

That's it, the momma bear in me was awakened! My decision was made. I was getting my studies done, getting a job, and putting the kids in daycare.

Almost a year-long battle followed my decision. We weren't on the same page. I needed to do this for the wellbeing of my boys, and nothing was going to stop me. One thing he knew about me was that when I decided on something, I would find a way to make it happen. The funny part was that I didn't recognize that trait in myself back then.

On the first day of daycare, I sat in the car with my boys in the back. I looked at them with tears of joy and nervousness. Their cute smiles filled my heart, and as I took them out of the car, I squeezed them into big hugs. This was going to help my boys. I dropped them off, and back in the car, I found my thoughts contradicting my actions.

Why can't he see that this is important? Why am I fighting alone?

I got it done; they will do great here!

I literally felt the invisible stars on my shoulders. As if I had accomplished something big here—and it was all thanks to me. It felt like I had proven a point, that the wellbeing of my kids was more important than money. Yet, this came at a different cost.

Money is a sensitive topic in many marriages. In mine, my subconscious belief that a man decides, and the wife follows, led me to give into situations where I should have said no. I finally became aware of this belief once I became a mother. My inner dynamic had changed forever. It wasn't only about providing for my husband anymore, now it was about providing for my children. I quickly realized that the value system that I held strongly was different from what my husband valued. Throughout our marriage, there were two big challenges, money and alcohol. I did not want these to be challenges passed down to my boys.

As a mother, I knew that I wouldn't be okay with my boys only finding relief in alcohol. Yet, I had to think in more depth here—why did their father believe that alcohol was an outlet? That is when I realized that at the age of 16, he was sent abroad. He had traveled the world at a very young age, with the task of making something out of himself and sending money back home to pay off the debt that was taken on to make this a reality for him. Can you imagine sending your 16-year-old boy off to another country with such a burdensome responsibility?

I couldn't then, and I can't even now!

It gives me chills just thinking about it. Yet, this is the reality for so many boys and girls. The intention of their parents is right, they want them to live a better life, but at what cost? Would he have chosen this path if there was no external pressure for him, and would he have had a better chance at succeeding if he valued education more? I simply don't know. All I can do is wonder what I would have done.

I imagined being in his shoes and in an ecosystem where alcohol was a norm. I saw myself being encouraged to study, but if I didn't, it was okay too. As a boy, you would figure it out. Would I leave my parents at the age of 16 to start fresh in a new country?

Then I asked myself questions that he hadn't been allowed to ask himself. What would he have done if he had a choice? Would he have chosen to really focus on his studies so he could make something of himself? Or would he still have worked and not completed his studies? Why did alcohol become a relief, a coping mechanism? And why was money more important than relationships? Why did he believe that he was only worthy if we sent money home? Was it truly the fault of the 16-year-old who didn't know better?

I can't say for sure what he thought. What I did know was that for so many years, men drank their sorrows away. He, too, saw this dynamic growing up, never questioning it, and in adulthood, but fully embracing it. This was his normal.

Reflecting on his past also made me question my own behavior. Why was I accepting unfair behavior? Growing up, I had seen that men decide what happens and the woman follows. This turned into a subconscious belief and somewhere I started thinking that my feelings were irrelevant, that I needed to listen to the men of the house to be a good woman.

Now that I have raised my understanding from both perspectives, what would I do? At the end of the day, we both had the freedom of choice, even if it didn't feel like a reality for me. We didn't have to agree with each other's life choices. Yet the important thing was to come to an understanding. This was missing big time for us both. I fought with the idea of divorce. Each day, I would put up a smile, but inside I was depressed. No one knew how I felt, not even my family.

Then, one day, things changed. He came home around 7 p.m., and I was sitting on the couch with one of my boys. As always, he would greet the boys, give them a quick hug and kiss, and then settle into his favorite side of the couch. Within 30 minutes, the alcohol would come out, and he would start watching TV to unwind. I can't remember what triggered an argument, but we started arguing, and he kept demeaning me. Angered, I walked away. Enough! I couldn't take this anymore. I wanted it to stop! This wasn't a marriage. It had become a prison and a poison of my own emotions.

The next day, I sat in the car, in the parking lot at work. I had intentionally parked further away, so that no one could see the tears that were flowing from my eyes. With a lot of courage, I started telling my sisters the horrors that I was living in. I couldn't take it anymore.

"Tell Dad," said my older sister.

"But how? What if he tells me to figure it out?" I said, crying.

"You can't leave him without telling Mom and Dad. Tell them!"

"Okay!" I said.

I needed to make the call right away before I talked myself out of it. I called Dad and just started crying. His concerning voice on the other side of the phone asked, "What is wrong? Are you okay?"

Once I calmed myself down, the words that came out of me sounded like: "I can't take this anymore, I can't stay with him! There are too many arguments and the daily emotional abuse is breaking me."

With my heart beating in my throat, I waited for his response. "Okay, what do you want to do?"

A sigh of relief left my body. *Thank God he didn't say that I needed to figure it out,* I thought.

Here I was, about to take the BIGGEST step of my life, leaving him, and my family was halfway across the globe, now worried about me. I had made arrangements to go home, grab my stuff, and then go to a women's shelter with my children. Once I got home, his parents didn't allow me to leave. They wanted us all to talk it out. That night, when he got home, he was shocked that I had been thinking of taking that step. When I told him that my father wanted to speak with him, something broke between us even more.

Dad, on the other side of the phone, started asking him, "What is going on?"

He looked at me with an angered look and said nothing at first. Then he said, "We can figure this out. Please don't worry."

Once he hung up, he looked at me and said, "Because of you, I have lost their respect today!"

I couldn't believe my ears—*because of me?*

It had been a long emotional day, I didn't have any energy left to go, so I stayed quiet.

The next morning, both our parents started talking about how we need to give it another chance. I was emotionally exhausted, and didn't know what to say. He started convincing me that he would do better and to give him another chance. So I did.

A few months after his parents went back to India, sitting at the opposite ends of the couch, I approached the conversation again.

"Can we please talk about what happened, and find a path forward if we really want to make it work?" I asked.

He looked at me, and said, "This is a hard part of our lives, but things will get better, just give me another chance."

A big part of me wanted me to believe him, and the uncertainty of life if I did leave him wasn't sexy either. "Okay, but we both have to make real effort in making this relationship work."

He agreed!

He started coming home earlier, drinking less, and to be more involved with the kids than just giving them a kiss and a hug. *Things are in a better place,* I thought. Until I got pregnant! Yes, it wasn't planned, but it happened. I am not sure how this put even more pressure on him, but that is what he felt, and so things went from good to worse.

We went from working on our relationship to once again being completely disconnected. He started staying out late again, coming home drunk. The emotional abuse took a heavy toll on me. Here I was, working a full-time job, taking care of my boys and pregnant. In a period of life where a woman is meant to be nurtured and showered with love, I was being depleted. In the parking lot of the grocery store, strangers would approach me to help me with the groceries, but my own husband didn't consider how I was doing it all.

I felt a deep sense of sorrow from within. The type of sorrow that robbed me from enjoying my pregnancy. I did what I could with a smile. My colleagues were worried about me, and even asked how I was still smiling and putting up with it all.

Do I have another choice? I thought.

During my 36-week pregnancy, we had an argument that escalated into physical abuse. That night I felt scared, scared for my boys, for the little girl inside of me and for the future. The next morning, I was still shaken by the experience but put on a smile, dropped off the boys at daycare and went to work. Knowing that my colleague was alone in the office, I went to her and shared what had happened.

With her beautiful, calm demeanor she said, "I am concerned for you. Who would take care of the kids if it wasn't for you?"

Those words hit hard! Yes, what would I do? No words were coming from my mouth, just tears flowing down.

She kindly calmed me down. "We have your baby shower tonight, so let's talk more after that."

I agreed.

With big smiles, hugs, and everything pink, I was welcomed at the baby shower. While on the inside, I was sad, I took in all the positivity and attention that I could at that moment. My friends had gone through much effort to make this a special occasion for me. I felt happy and safe there. After the party, a few of my friends stayed back and shared their concern for me and my children. Their words woke up what I already knew from deep within. I needed to leave him! I stayed away for a week.

As my due date was nearing, I was getting nervous about doing it all on my own. I chose to go back to him, as he had been pleading for another chance. Not to make my marriage work again, but to focus on what was the most important thing, which was the delivery of my girl. I can't tell you how often I prayed for a better solution, to just make it another day for the sake of my children.

A few weeks after my daughter was born, I received a phone call. My blessing, I call it!

The voice on the other side of the call said, "You have been looking for a place, and we believe we have the best solution for you."

I was quiet for a second, and quickly said, "Tell me more!" God had answered my prayer. A solution, my light at the end of the tunnel was here!

My parents tried to convince me to come home to the Netherlands, and while I wanted to, I said no. "I can't take my babies away from their dad, my relationship is ending, not theirs!" I kept saying. My parents, my sisters, my friends – they all came together and held me up at a time when I thought I was going to break down. I was seen, supported, and heard.

When my daughter was exactly a month old, I moved out. Tears of relief flowed from my eyes. He knew I was leaving that day and still texted me asking if I was making dinner before leaving. That was my sign, it confirmed for me that my decision to leave was the right one!

But I didn't go back to the Netherlands, I chose to create a new home for me and my children. I recognized that my inner child needed my parents' approval to leave him. The parental instinct however didn't want me to become the reason that he didn't have a relationship with his own children. So I stayed in the same city and didn't move back to the Netherlands, where all my family lived. I knew that my relationship had ended, but my children would always be connected to him. While it was a very logical decision, it was also what made me dig deeper in my own healing journey.

Why, then, was I still miserable and doubting my choices after all I had been through? I had peace, safety, laughter, a place to call my home— what else did I want or need? Inside, I was still missing something. A sense of deeper peace and love for myself. Something that I never cultivated. Not knowing how to get to a deeper inner peace, I looked up to the ceiling and asked God for guidance. "Show me the way…" I begged.

God delivered.

I started watching *Tony Robbins* on YouTube, invested in myself through various programs, invested in events which helped me be a better mom, and slowly but surely, I got to a moment where deeper inner peace became my essence.

The biggest lesson was that I had never asked myself what Matina wanted. I was always living someone else's agenda, and I did it with love. That's all I had known until I understood that self-love is more important. Yes, it is more important because I believe my marriage didn't work due to lack of self-love.

If I don't love myself, how could I have love for my partner? If I am not happy with who I am and how I am living, then how could I find happiness in my partner? I recognized that all the internal questions that I had all along were my inner guidance speaking to me—asking me to find myself first. I heard the inner questions, but never understood the essence of them. Gosh, I had so many moments of self-reflection but so many questions were based on others, not myself. Now, I ask myself first, what do I want?

I also started seeing my marriage in a different light. Two souls who were disconnected from themselves had come together, following the external drivers and not recognizing the importance of self-reflection. My reflection gave me a deeper understanding of why he was the way he was.

I could still hear his words ringing in my ears, "You are stupid!" Words that have a certain energy, and these were out to hurt me internally. What I hadn't recognized was that hearing those words daily, broke my inner spirit and brought an insecure Matina to life.

How could someone want to deliberately hurt you when they claim they love you?.

Well, the answer wasn't something I was willing to see then, but what I recognize now. He was hurting and, for whatever reason, he felt he could only express it negatively.

Did I accept it? Yes, I did. Do I now? No, I don't!

I recognize that the lack of self-worth was causing me to accept the behavior. My inner work raised my self-worth to a level which was unknown to me during my marriage. All the self-reflection gave me peace and the ability to forgive and let go. What I learned is that forgiveness isn't for the other person, it is for my inner peace as well as self-forgiveness.

My marriage taught me a lot, my divorce taught me even more! The Matina of today feels liberated from the inside, and I feel privileged to share my lessons with others. I recognized that even while my marriage didn't last. I did love him, and I didn't have to call that love wrong because it didn't work out. I value myself for the heart that I have and the care that I show. Don't call your heart wrong!

These words spoke to my heart in those moments...

"Lose You To Love Me" by Selena Gomez

You promised the world and I fell for it
I put you first and you adored it
Set fires to my forest
And you let it burn
Sang off-key in my chorus
'Cause it wasn't yours
I saw the signs and I ignored it
Rose-colored glasses all distorted
Set fire to my purpose
And I let it burn
You got off on the hurtin'
When it wasn't yours, yeah
We'd always go into it blindly
I needed to lose you to find me
This dancing was killing me softly
I needed to hate you to love me, yeah
I needed to lose you to love me
And now the chapter is closed and done
And now it's goodbye, it's goodbye for us

Matina Singh is a holistic healer, life coach, and motivational speaker based in Canada. After going through her divorce and heartbreak, Matina discovered her spiritual gifts and passion for helping others heal and rediscover themselves. She specializes in divorce recovery coaching, emotion code practitioner, and holistic healing practices. Matina believes that everyone has something unique to offer the world and has the power within them to rebuild their lives. Her mission is to shine a light on the abilities that her clients have hidden within themselves and guide them to their best lives. She uses spiritual practices, energy work, and coaching techniques to help her clients overcome personal barriers, rediscover their inner strength, and strengthen their relationships. Matina's journey through her divorce and path of self-discovery has given her deep insights and compassion that she brings to her work empowering others.

Unwritten

PRIYA KAUR TAHIM

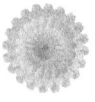

"If you make a mistake, you sit down, apologize and take what comes your way. If you didn't do anything wrong, you stand up and fight for yourself like the lioness you are."

These words, loosely translated from Punjabi to English, were told to me by my Nani—my maternal grandmother. My Nani has constantly shown me what it means to be a strong, courageous woman. She taught me to not only live life with morals, rules, and values, but to stand up for what is right. To fight for my voice. The number of times these words played through my head when I was trying to leave *you* cannot be counted or measured.

Nobody gets married and thinks it will end up with two strangers parting ways. This isn't a story about loss. This is a story about falling in love. This story isn't about a version of us, but it is about *me and you*. There was never an us, there was always just *me and you*, two souls that intertwined for a moment in time, operating on very different wavelengths.

I remember my younger self didn't believe in divorce. I remember judging people for "quitting" or "giving up" when things got tough. A part of me still holds marriage as a higher power—worth the investment and sacrifice. But at what cost?

Life showed me.

Growing up as a Sikh woman with two sisters, we were taught from a young age that family was everything. We were taught to prioritize building close-knit relationships with our grandparents, cousins, aunts and uncles—regardless of us living many oceans away. This is something that I cannot thank my parents enough for instilling in us, as the bonds we share are unlike any I know.

I never imagined myself having to battle my love for family and the blind love I shared for *you*. I never thought I'd be forced to choose between the two. For as long as I could remember, I imagined myself finding a partner that melted into my family dynamic, excited to enjoy Friday night pizzas, or random tava sessions with my family. Little did I know, that was what I craved the most when I could no longer have it.

When *you* made me feel like I was nothing, I'd remind myself that I can do it. I'd imagine my mom's strength and think to myself that this was normal. Feeling small was normal. It wasn't. It isn't. No one should have to experience what I went through. I wish I could tell the younger version of my mom that as well. I know our situations were different, but I fought, and now share my story for her, along with everyone else who felt like their voice didn't matter. This story is ours.

You've been matched!

That notification on my phone still plays through my mind. Who could imagine that a tiny, insignificant notification in May 2015 could turn my life into a cyclone. I remember that first phone call during which *you* painted this picture of your life. Everything about *you* seemed so mature, grown-up and intentional. *You* had passions, hobbies, excitement. And most importantly, *you* had a routine.

Laying on the sofa, across from my little sister, I was excited to share with her that "he's so well-rounded, cute, and tall." The butterflies set in shortly after our first 20-minute phone call, which turned into days of continuous texting, video chatting and calling.

It wasn't long before my days revolved around *you*.

I'm still so angry at myself for allowing time to become limited with individuals who were physically present. I became consumed with *your* love. In a blink of an eye, I went from being surrounded by friends to being surrounded by *you* and only *you*.

My whole life I've been blessed with amazing people who love and care about me. These people have not only helped shape me into who I am today, but they've also influenced me to push myself to be the person I want to be. I've grown up believing in sayings like, "Everything happens for a reason," and "Live your life to the fullest". Even after all the trauma I've experienced in my life, I still believe that everything happens for a reason, and that certain people come into your life for a greater good.

Growing up, I had three male influences that helped shape who I've become: My Dad, *Papaji* (Paternal Grandfather) and *Nanaji* (Maternal Grandfather). All three of these men aligned in the values of creating a sense of independence and the importance of family. My dad, although he was always traveling, taught us that hard work pays off. He embraced the importance of being financially independent, not having to rely on others. My *Papaji's* legacy was that all his kids, grandchildren, and great-grandchildren received an education. Papaji's goal was that we all were able to take care of ourselves and in his eyes education was the key. My *Nanaji* taught me that no matter what life throws your way, you embrace it with a smile and strength. One of the last things he said to me was "ask for as much love as your heart desires and share it with the world."

Much like my male role models, I've grown up with some of the strongest women I know. My mom is the definition of a superwoman. She ensured that my sisters and I never felt a lack of support, and she showed us that strength comes from within. I see that now, as an adult, but as a child, I remember feeling like her support was focused more on my sisters than me. My older sister needed my mom more growing up and this caused my mom to give her extra attention naturally (well, what I felt like at the time was more attention), which made me independent. I rarely relied on anyone. At the age of 14, my freshman year of high school, I got a job at Kumon, an after-school math and reading program. I generally made decisions on my own, and rarely went to people for advice. Instead, I'd be the one people came to for advice.

Sometimes when I needed someone to talk to, I felt like I couldn't go to my mom. Looking back, as an adult, I'm sure that wasn't the case, but I remember feeling like I had to fight battles alone. This feeling placed a strain on my mother's relationship with me. She seemed to think I was jealous and I seemed to think that she didn't care. Honestly, it was a big misunderstanding.

I think that a part of being the younger sister is feeling left out. My relationship with my little sister has always been turbulent. I think a lot of animosity develops when our perceptions are skewed. Growing up, my younger sister and I fought like crazy, but it wasn't out of the ordinary. I am so incredibly proud of my sister for becoming the actual, independent woman she is today; however, I wish I could turn back time and tell her how much she meant to me. Being the middle child, I never felt like I fit in. I felt like my older sister thrived in her role as "didi", and my younger sister thrived in her role as the "baby." I never understood that you could have a close relationship with both siblings, without having to sacrifice one for the other. Maybe that's why I had so much difficulty managing my relationship with you and them. Maybe that's why it's so hard to rebuild a relationship as an adult. I always say, it's never too late to build a bond, but you can't go back and recreate something.

My dad was my best friend. When I met *you*, it changed everything. I momentarily lost that relationship with my dad, and that is something I hate. I hate *you*, but more importantly, I hate myself for allowing that to happen. How could I give up one of the most important relationships for someone who was supposed to love all of me, not parts of me.

My dad doesn't like to be the center of attention, unlike my sisters and mom, who love to be social butterflies. I like to say I'm a perfect blend of personalities between my parents: an introverted extrovert. When it comes to being outgoing and social, I'm more like my mom. My mom loves to throw parties and family gatherings. She loves to cook and entertain. One thing about my mom is she never says "no." No matter what state of mind she's in, or if she's physically not feeling well, she's always there for everyone. She's a carbon copy of her dad, and I admire the strength she has. My mom will never admit the strength she's had to endure, or the pain she's had to experience. I see how much life has thrown at her, and whenever I feel like I can't handle something—I channel my mom's strength.

I remember how seamlessly we intertwined, or what I felt like was seamless at the time.   Everything was moving really fast, sort of like a movie. Intro, plot, climax, conclusion—all within a month. We went from talking on the phone and falling in love to meeting and family introductions all within a 45-day timespan.

You showed me the world on a silver platter, which turned out to be a silver paper plate. Pretty on the outside, but not durable. The feelings I had, picking you up at the airport were indescribable. *You* were wearing a salmon-colored dress shirt, which made me think about Ross in *Friends*. *You* were supposed to be my lobster. That weekend is still one of my favorite memories. Being giddy, playing tourist in my own city, going on never-ending dates… it was like having a sleepover with my bestie. *You* played on my emotions and empathy. This was supposed to be my weekend. It was supposed to revolve around me; it was my birthday, after all. I remember *you* were supposed to leave after one day, but you extended *your* trip to celebrate my sister's 21st birthday. I felt so lucky to have met someone that finally understood the importance of family. God, I was dumb. Even on that weekend, so many things went wrong.

I remember having the time of my life, celebrating my sister's birthday and my own with all my favorite people. That was until *you* made me feel guilty. Playing on my emotions, saying "I feel overwhelmed, I need to go home." Even in that moment, I couldn't understand what was overwhelming *you*, but I gave *you* the benefit of doubt. I left my sister's 21st birthday to take care of *you*. I picked *you* over her, and that slowly became the pattern. I always picked *you*.

Then it happened a few short weeks later. My dad saw your truth. Saw your aura, and questioned your motive. How could I miss all the red flags? How could I have misjudged reality so much? I remember our first fight about my dad's reaction to meeting *you*. He treated *you* with so much respect, he was being protective, but he never once treated *you* like a stranger. Any good dad wants what's best for his daughter. He had every right to question *your* intent with wanting to be with me. Was it because of *your* citizenship (or lack thereof), or because *you* wanted me? I'll admit, I never could understand why it couldn't be both, but maybe that's my ignorance. I used to be so proud of my ignorance, mainly because I always choose to see the good in others, and light in dark places.

I was willing to give *you* my world for the world *you* presented to me. But *you* couldn't even give me an ounce back. Everything was always a struggle. Every question was a fight. Every need was a disappointment. Every moment was a delusion. Even after choosing *you* from the start, it was not enough. It was never enough.

I remember writing this email to you, begging you for things that shouldn't have even been a question.

I love you, and we will fight through this. There are things you're gonna have to do for me that you don't like, just like there are things I have to do that I don't like. I love you, you love me. We want to be together and we will be. We have to stay strong, communicate, and never turn against each other.

I'm being rational. I'm ready to leave my comfort behind, and with a smile because I have you by my side, please understand and try to meet me there. I love you. Believe in us. Don't let others fill our head with doubts.

You're my rock. My best friend. My hero. But most importantly, you're my partner, which means....you and me, we are together, side by side. I can't wait to lie in your arms tomorrow night.

Love you. Don't be mad. I just needed to say this before I slept. Call me when you're home!

Pri's iPhone

This was month two. Two months into a relationship should be the honeymoon phase, but we were planning our future, or what I imagined it to be. Maybe I was delusional to think *your* words were real. Maybe I was delusional to think *you'd* protect me from all the monsters and storms that were about to come my way. But how could *you* protect me when *you* were both the monster and storm?

I wish I could give that version of me a big hug and protect her from the scars she was about to uncover. I wish I could take away all the pain. But at the same time, I want to tell her the pain will make her into the strong woman she becomes. I want to tell her she will never let the pain become her identity instead, she allowed it to be a part of her story.

It wasn't long until I lost myself in the chaos of *your temper*. I found myself making excuses for all *your* faults, and telling my loved ones it was all okay. *You* were worth it. I find myself looking at this version, full of doubt, shame and fear – like a stranger I never knew.

I remember fighting my parents for *you*. It's still so clear, as if it was yesterday. The hurt in my dad's eyes when I told him "I'd run away to be with *you*." This was only the beginning. This was only the start of *you* becoming my whole world, and me being a pawn in *yours*.

There were moments I can remember where I felt like the center of *your* universe, but that's just it… the center of *your* universe, not '*our* universe.' Everything revolved around how *you* felt, how you perceived the situation, and how wronged in *your* life *you've been*. But how can everyone in *your* life disappoint you? At some point, isn't it also a possibility that *you* thrive on being the wronged one? Life isn't always full of color, but it also can't all be so gloomy.

I remember countless nights, where I would cry myself to sleep because I wasn't enough *for you*. You always failed to recall the moments I put *you* first, instead you focused on the few times I fought for small moments for me. I still feel the aches of the voiceless cries, and the tears that flooded my eyes. I craved being hugged and being told it would be ok in those moments. Instead, I was met with *your* back to my face, or loud shouts telling me how much of a "child" I was. I craved the validation that *you* were just angry and that *you* didn't mean the pain you caused.

Every fight became more and more explosive—yet we never discussed what led me to break down or attempt to walk away. *Your* excuse was always that *you* "didn't force me" to do anything, whenever I would try to share how I was feeling. Writing seemed to be the only medium where I could say my point, but even then *you* never heard me, and that never changed. Instead, *you* would fight back with me.

I didn't force you to walk out of the apartment. I didn't ask you not to take your keys. As a smart adult, you should have thought about that yourself. It's your apartment too and you can come home or leave when you want. Don't blame me for it. I'm tired of you emailing and saying whatever you want. Every single thing you said is just plain wrong.

Best Regards,
You

Both of us are not at fault. I see zero remorse in you for any of the things listed above. That is utterly disgusting. I am angry because you do exactly what I tell you we can't afford. You disrespect me. You refuse to be a married couple. A married couple makes financial decisions together, not alone. Anything I have ever bought, I have told you about, never hid it. I have sold everything that I don't use to buy my new gear. And that gear is for my dream. For something that I feel I was born to do.

Landing a second job when your first one isn't paying bills is not an accomplishment. It's your goddamn job to make sure you help with finances. You should have been doing Uber, Lyft, working anywhere and everywhere you can to make sure our ends meet. You act like you are doing me a favor by getting a second job. You could have had a second job a long time ago, it didn't have to be with counseling. But you chose to sit at home and watch TV, and work for two hours a day. Yeah, I sit at home too and become lazy, but the only reason I do that is because I get a good damned salary... no matter what. If I was in your position, I would NEVER be seen at home. No matter how sick, no matter how tired I was. I started DJing again. I started selling mixing/mastering gigs online. I started calling anyone and everyone I know to get more gigs so that we can stay afloat.

Until you feel remorse for what you did, until you understand that finances are above everything, until you understand that going to Dallas is the dumbest decision you can make: for financial reasons, for our health as a couple, and for yourself as an individual woman; you're right. You will not be good enough for me... until you understand all of the above. I've had it with your dependent nature on family. It's childish, it's a disgusting crutch and it needs to be removed. You never learned to live on your own and be strong. You never learned what it means to be a strong, independent individual. I loved a woman who was independent. Who said she would be willing to grow with me, financially and without family and focus on each other and our future businesses, our fitness etc. Not whoever you have become. You didn't give up your career. Don't ever say that to me. You fucked up when we were in Dallas. You allowed your family to intervene in our lives. You refused to understand who I was and how important it is to remain away from family to grow as a couple. That is the reason I am depressed, because of your lack of understanding. And that is the reason we had to move so soon.

You didn't give up your career, you are working in it right now in the same damn career. The past few months have been financially bad not because you had to start over, but because you made poor decisions about when to go to the ER, when to seek doctor's help, and when to not buy Dallas tickets and a Kate Spade bag.

Priya

You think having a shared private practice and a $50K job with minimal health insurance = 'Dream Job'? That's just sad. I feel bad for you because you have thought up this lie to yourself. A dream job is worth $500,000.... and a building you know.... that's a dream job. You throw the fact that we left Dallas in my face like I made you do something you didn't want to, it's disgusting.

You

Family—You NEED family? Then you will never truly have me. We have tried many things, but you ultimately always justify your actions by "But I love my family and it's my support". A healthy marriage is never achieved until the

spouse becomes the "need." They are always number one.
I have supported you over anything else since we have
been married. Never once jeopardized our finances or our
relationship to go see Mom or to agree with my family.
You do this on a regular basis. You will finally grow up
when you can look me in the eye and tell me that you don't
"need" family. You give me all these lectures in your email
about vows and marriage. I have never been more in tune
with the promises I made. Not once have I put you second.
Or thrown away a decision that we made together. I can
honestly say that you are so lucky to have me. Not for once
in my life, however, have I felt like I fucking matter in your
life, which revolves around your family/friends and your
deluded views on what you are doing. You keep deluding
yourself into thinking, "What else is going on?". You keep
asking me that. You fail to understand the gravity of the
situation that you have put us in. That is what is going on.
We are not seeing a marriage counselor. The simple reason
is that when I asked you to see one, you said "no." I see
no remorse in your email about what you did. And that
proves to me, you don't understand the situation. I hope
you understand someday, but that's not today.

Best Regards,
You

Every point I tried to make, turned into a malicious version of somehow
me taking advantage of *you* or being avoidant to *your* opinions. It never
mattered. No matter how hard I tried to be the version of *me* that *you*
wanted.

The crippling pain of how unloved and unattractive *you* made me feel,
eventually led me into a world of depressive cycles and feeling numb.
My laugh no longer had a giggle, my smile no longer appeared bright.
I wanted so badly to feel something. I would crave moments of being
delusional that *we were happy*. That's the thing. We *were* happy…in
fleeting moments.

We built an empire. It appeared we created a lifestyle we both envisioned, only it wasn't. How could I let *you* alter my dreams? How did I allow my dreams of what I wanted out of life to be so easily melted into the version of *your* dream? Was buying multiple homes, traveling, investing, building financial freedom, something I wanted? Yes. BUT that wasn't all I wanted. I yearned to be loved in a way where my dreams mattered. I wanted to create a family with *you*. I wanted us to blend our families together. I was delusional to think that would ever happen. How could it when *you* created a wall, blocking that from the moment we got married. Not even six months into marriage, *you* isolated me from the people that meant the most to me by sending them this email, without my consent.

Family,

I'm emailing this and not saying this in person because I'm truly trying to avoid communication issues because of emotions. I know what happened yesterday came out of a place of love from the family. But, it was not a conversation I wanted to have with my family. I know Priya is your daughter/sister, but she is also my wife. And I don't think Priya and I will ever be able to build a trusting relationship if she leans on family every time something goes wrong with us, and everyone comes to our rescue. So, I'm asking for help. I am respectfully requesting you all to please avoid coming to the apartment every time Priya reaches out and says we are having issues. I want us to work through this by ourselves. I really hope this is not taken the wrong way, I'm just trying to do what I think is best for my marriage. I know Priya and I will be fine because even though we fight, we do love each other very much, and I hope things become more amicable between the rest of the family. I have done my best to make sure I don't lose my sanity while trying to keep the family happy. Unfortunately, it hasn't worked and now it's time to focus on Priya and me, more than anything else.

Hope everyone has a happy Thanksgiving.

with love,
You

As always, it was never discussed what led me to reach out for help. There was no mention of the emotional abuse, threats to leave, physically packing bags and the yelling… I don't wish it on my worst enemy to ever experience the other end of *your* yelling. The sound, the tone, the words…each one stabbing me deeper and deeper, until no more pain was felt. It became a norm. I saw something one way, you saw it a different way, I was told I was wrong followed by hours of yelling attacking my character, appearance, lack of communication skills, inability to love, my family bonds… everything that made me who I was.

We'd have these explosive arguments, where I'd end up bawling on the floor waiting to be hugged. I'd crave just being told I was loved. Then we'd promise to never let it get this bad again, that *we* were in this for the long haul and *our* love mattered. We'd have these grand conversations about how we wanted our future to look. At times, it was clear, the two of us against the world. Other times, it was like we were operating on two different Marvel timelines. It's ironic, we had such a comforting routine: watching The Office or a Marvel movie, playing video games, exploring—but all of that was superficial. The stuff that really mattered, didn't matter to *you*, and in turn didn't feel like it mattered to me.

You were consumed by *your* dream to become a celebrity. That was *your* focal point. Everything revolved around the success of your music, not only in our marriage, but in your relationships with others. No relationship was safe if *your* music wasn't respected or admired in the way *you* envision. *Your* expectations were impossible. I couldn't live up to them, and *you* couldn't live up to them either.

I think I always knew that this wasn't my happily ever after, but I was ashamed. I fought for *you*. I loved *you* with every part of me. I wanted so badly to be *your* world. I tried to stay. I tried to leave. No matter how many times I tried, I failed.

Finally, I watched as my family blended together on a family trip, where both sides of my family (Mom and Dad's) were able to enjoy each other's company without limitations. I observed everyone laughing, singing, dancing, and I found myself aching. *Why weren't we enough for you? Why couldn't you join me and have fun with me in front of my family? Why did it always just have to be the two of us? Why did I have to choose between you or them?*

I thought I was battling this pain solo and that I had made it through the trip, until my *Mamaji* pulled me aside on our last night. Without even saying a word, I broke down. I allowed my tears to flood and my pain to be freed. I felt safe. I didn't feel judged. I was able to see that I was allowed to have it all. I was allowed to experience happiness, both as a couple and as a family. I was allowed to be loved and love in return.

It was the first time in a while that I chose to love myself. The day after I got back from my trip, I remember thinking, *"if you loved me, you'd embrace me when I got home."* Again, I craved the delusion that my biggest fear wouldn't come true. My fear of losing *you*, but the truth is, *you* were never mine. Instead, I was met with anger, hours of yelling and being told how brainwashed I am. *You* told me I was not normal for having fun with my family and not you. *You* yelled at me for five hours and 34 minutes straight. Not one word in from me. That was the day I gained my strength and decided to leave. I met with a lawyer, I told my brother-in-law my plan (because everyone else was done with my delusion of actually leaving) and I'd be free finally.

Only, I stayed...again. I kept hoping that this was a nightmare, and that *you'd* be the man I thought *you* were. There were moments I could see *you* trying. I saw hope. It was again me living in a world of my own delusion.

Hey *You*,

I wanted to write out my feelings because every time I try to talk them out loud, I either can't get the words out, or I just shut down. I hope that you can read this and we can talk about it tomorrow after work, to give us both some time to collect our thoughts.

I am thankful for how hard you are trying the past three weeks. I know it hasn't been easy for you, either. I know you feel like a lot of your needs are not met, and I know I also feel that way. I love you very much and it is really hard to muster the courage to say this.

My love for you is so strong, that for so long I've just sacrificed being unhappy. I came back in March, thinking that we would be able to work things out. Thinking we would be able to be stronger than our love. Truth is, sometimes love isn't always enough.

Priya

I continue to realize how unhappy I am, and I realized how severely unhappy I was when I wasn't even excited about Christmas. I always put up the tree the day after Thanksgiving, but this year I just can't. I am not in a good place, and I believe that's because I have been putting this conversation off for so long. I can't imagine my life without you, but I also know that I can't go on like this. I am so broken. I get physically sick thinking about losing you, but also staying in a position where I feel so broken.

You once asked me why I get sad when you enter the room—it's not that I get sad. It's because I have been battling this inner demon of how attached I am to you. I'm so attached that I don't even recognize myself anymore.

I don't laugh as much, I don't enjoy doing anything I used to, and I also don't remember the last time I went a day without anxiety.

I don't want to make this harder than it already is. I love you and I want you to be happy. You are my everything, but I am not happy. I really want you to find your happiness and shine like the star I know you are. I don't want to argue or fight anymore. I have been thinking about this for a long time, about how unhappy I am and how unhappy I make you.

I think we should divorce/separate and continue to support each other. I think it's best to do this when we aren't fighting, but simply being realistic and rational. You are my best friend, and I hope we can continue to be as we navigate things.

I enjoy your company so much and love you with everything-that's why it's been so hard for me to even share how unhappy I've been. My hope is that you can understand where I'm coming from, and work with me to be the best separated partners we can be. I hope we can work together to separate and enjoy moments together still as we work to establish our new norm.

I love you and I'm sorry for hurting you the way I have. You deserve more and I know that I am not enough for you.

Love always,
Your Priya

I never could've predicted the unraveling of *us* that was to follow this olive branch. I took responsibility for it all, despite the truth that, in fact, this wasn't just me. Despite the fact that I was a great partner and supportive spouse. I played the role of wife well. I owned the roles I played, even though the roles were defined for me by *you*. I owned the sleepless nights that were caused by your rage. I still find myself in awe of the colors that bled as *you* revealed yourself. "If I could, I would kill your family." The words haunt me and probably will for the rest of my life. It wasn't about the reality of *your* statement; it was about how the thought could even cross *your* mind. That's when I knew, it was now or never. Calling my dad, full of shame, fear, and defeat, vomiting all the pain and horror I'd been living. And, just like that, I had my family back. My dad, the unsung hero he is, gave me the strength to come home.

I am more than my scars, pain, fear, and shame. I am me and I wear that honor proudly. I am no longer the girl who had no voice. I fell in love with myself throughout this healing journey. I may not be where I thought I would be in life, but I am on my way.

This story is just the beginning, the rest is still unwritten...

Priya Kaur Tahim, is a Licensed Professional Counselor and National Certified Counselor in Washington, D.C., Virginia and Texas-as well as founder of Kaur Counseling, children's book author, Podcast host and avid traveler. Priya found her passion in helping others find their voice, at a young age-which stemmed into her career as a therapist and practice owner.

Priya earned her MA in Professional Counseling from Amberton University in Garland, TX and received her BA in Psychology from Texas Woman's University in Denton, TX.

Fun fact: Priya loves to dance, create new recipes in the kitchen, and travel/explore new places. She is also obsessed with her nieces and coffee/tea.

Never Settle... Even If You Are Older

SABRINA KAUR

I was 25 when I thought I had it all. An education, a good job, my own house, and a brand-new car. But I'm a Punjabi girl, and Punjabi girls have to get married. So even though I felt I had accomplished more than most other women my age—especially other Punjabi girls—I was led to believe that my actual accomplishment was yet to come, securing a good marital alliance.

Those other Punjabi girls were born and bred for marriage, and I didn't believe they would amount to much in life. Who even wants to be a housewife with no education and pop out some kids? Definitely not me. I'm different. I'm unique. I'm not born and bred for marriage. I had my whole life ahead of me. I had to move up in the corporate world; I had to travel the globe; I had to invest in more real estate; I had to make more money. That was my focus.

My mother and society had other ideas for me. Now that I was 25, the pressure to get married was on. My mother had pushed me into being a high achiever, pushed me towards university, pushed me into a career, and now she began pushing me towards marriage. My mother had started with strict criteria for my future husband. He had to be Punjabi, Sikh, Jatt, and from the Malwa region of Punjab. I'm not sure why it mattered that he had to be from Malwa, since I was born and raised in Canada, but that was important to my mother.

My parents have been married nearly 50 years. I can't say it has been a fairy tale, as it was arranged. My dad had come to Canada at the age of 21 and went back to India at the age of 25 to get married. He was introduced to a few different girls and chose one that he thought was the prettiest. He and my mom hadn't even had a conversation with each other when they were arranged to get married. They were married within twenty days of first seeing each other. Shortly after my parents' wedding, my dad went back to Canada. My mom came to Canada about six months after she married my dad. Suddenly, it was just the two of them. There were some relatives nearby, but his parents and siblings were all in India.

My grandparents visited Canada for a few months when I was four years old. But they preferred their village in India and decided to go back. They never visited Canada again. Other than those few months and a couple of visits to India, my mother, unlike most married Indian women, never had to deal with living with in-laws. Which is why she never could have prepared me for all that I would experience when I got married.

My Nani (my mother's mother) actually lived with us for half the year and the remaining half of the year in India with my Mamma ji's family (mom's brother's family). So, in my household, my dad was the one who lived with an in-law. I could tell he didn't really love it, but it's not the same as a woman living with her husband's family and her husband's mother like I did, and so many Indian women do.

Going into my own marriage, I had no idea what it was going to be like living with in-laws, and an Indian mother-in-law.

I started to find out before the marriage began. During our wedding festivities, the start of a red-flag-infested journey that began, and got me questioning everything girls like me were taught.

Day one of my wedding week had finally arrived. This is the day every Desi girl dreams of—the marigold decor, the yellows, the soft pinks, the pink Punjabi *salwar kameez*, the makeup and hair done. My mother frantically ran around in the kitchen, making sure there was cha, pakoras, sweets, and other Indian snacks ready for all the ladies when they arrived. My parents' house was finally looking like a wedding house. It was starting to feel real now. I saw the look on my dad's face. He was beaming. His firstborn was finally getting married at 36 years old. My mother, although frantic and in her usual anxious state, was also happy as she laughed with guests. Even all of my aunts looked genuinely happy for once. Most importantly, I was feeling happy. It was finally my time. This was the moment I had been waiting for my entire life. I had been praying this day would come for the past twenty plus years while trying to play it cool. This was a bigger deal to me than any of my previous accomplishments. Getting those degrees, buying real estate, having a career—none of those seemed to be as important as this. I WAS GETTING MARRIED!

My aunt began reading the *Sukhmani Sahib*. Twenty women were all sitting on the floor of our living room, *chunnis* covering their heads. My cousins would join us soon too. Just in time for the mehndi artists. Taking in the scene, my mind began to wonder. In a few days, I will be married and living with my husband. Life will be great. I remember having the biggest smile on my face. I exchanged glances with several other women in the room, each giving me an approving and loving smile back.

We were only a few minutes into the *paath* when my phone began to ring. My future mother-in-law was calling. She must be calling to ask about some details for the wedding day, I had thought. Several of my fiancé's family members had called or texted me in the past couple days regarding last minute wedding details, so I didn't think her calling me now would be out of the ordinary. I quickly got up, stepped into the garage, and answered the call.

"Sat Sri Akal," I answered enthusiastically. She answered, *"Sat Sri Akal,"* back in a more serious and coarse tone. She did not sound happy. I asked her how she was, and she immediately told me how she was not feeling well. I asked her what was wrong. She answered back in a broken voice in Punjabi, "I'm stressed, no one is helping me here, I don't know what to do." I was confused. Why was she calling to tell me that? Did

she want me to help her with something?

I asked her more about what was going on. She began to tell me that she had no one at home to help with all the preparations for the wedding. I really did not know what to think while she was telling me all this. I knew they had hired a lady to help out in the kitchen, I didn't know what was going on between her and the sister-in-law. Maybe she just called to vent? So I tried to reassure her and told her things would be fine. She broke down. She began to complain more about her family members, her sons, and the short amount of time to prepare for this wedding. She told me she couldn't sleep at night and was on anti-anxiety pills. She said this wedding was too much for her. That felt like a jab at me. I remember I just kept telling her everything would be alright, I could tell she was crying a bit, and I tried to console her as best as I could. During that conversation, she did not once ask how I was doing, how the wedding preparations were going on my side, or what I was even doing at that time she called. She had no interest or care that it was my mehndi day and that we were in the middle of *Sukhmani Sahib paath*. She was only concerned with her own feelings.

I came back to the living room and sat down with all of my aunts. I wasn't smiling anymore. I was confused, I wasn't sure what to think. It seemed so odd to me that she would call me and complain about her relatives and how stressed she was about the wedding during our first day of events. I decided to shrug it off and not think about it too much. Little did I know that phone call set the tone for how living with my in-laws would be.

One week had gone by since our wedding. We just returned from a week away for our mini-honeymoon. One of the reasons why I wanted a husband and life partner was to have a life companion, a best friend, who I would travel and see the world with. My whole life, I was told that you can do whatever you want once you are married. When you are married, you can travel anywhere you want. When you are married, you can buy whatever you want. When you are married is when your life begins. Here I was thinking my life was just starting at 36. But I was mistaken. I was about to head into the most difficult time of my life.

We arrived back at his home, which was now our home. My mother-in-law was waiting anxiously and ran to my husband as soon as we came through the front door. His younger brother was not far behind. They both hugged my husband ever so tightly and gave me an awkward hug as well. I wanted to get settled in the house and prepare for the upcoming week.

The next morning, my alarm abruptly woke me at 6 a.m. At first, when I opened my eyes, I didn't quite know where I was. There were trees outside the window, and I remember thinking, that is so odd. I've never seen those trees before. It took me a few seconds to realize I was in my new bedroom, laying down next to my sleeping husband. I made my way downstairs to find my husband making me toast and eggs, just how I like my breakfast in the morning. My mother-in-law was also awake and making chai. We exchanged glances and I said good morning, in a dazed state. I remember she gave me a weird look and said good morning back, asking if I wanted chai. I don't normally drink chai, so I politely told her I'll make my own coffee. She didn't say anything. My husband excitedly set up my breakfast plate and coffee. I happily ate my breakfast and drank my coffee. This was nice, I felt lucky. I left the house, said goodbye to my husband. My mother-in-law had gone upstairs.

I came home later that evening. Traffic had been a nightmare. My husband suggested that we go to Costco and buy our groceries and get our toiletries. Perfect, I thought. Since I was hungry, and it was almost dinner time, we stopped for some food on the way to Costco. We went through Costco, filled our cart with all the foods I liked, meats, bread, vegetables, fruits, large packages of shampoo, conditioner, body wash, makeup remover, toothpaste, etc. We were doing husband/wife things, and it felt nice. We were setting up our home.

When we arrived home, my mother-in-law was there. I greeted her and told her we went to Costco. She curiously looked at all the stuff we had got. She immediately noticed the package of body wash, which came in a pack of three. She yelled, "We already have this!" Taken aback, I looked at her blankly. She went on to tell me we already have this in the laundry room. If you looked, you would have known. Apparently, she and the younger brother went to Costco once a week to stock up on toiletries. The younger brother also joined in. His voice was very loud and abrasive. At that moment, I wasn't quite sure how to react, so all I said was, "Ok, I didn't know." "Well, next time look!" replied my brother-in-law, ever so rudely. I quickly put away all the groceries. I looked at my husband, who had not said a word.

My husband finally came upstairs an hour later, with a concerned look on his face. He told me he had been talking to his mom and brother. His mom informed him that she was upset from the night before because I had not gone downstairs to sit with her. She also didn't like that I hadn't properly greeted her in the morning. I was anxious about going back to work and my new commute to work. On top of that, she said I should have checked to see what we had at home before I went to Costco. My husband told me that in the evenings, his mother wants us all to sit together and watch TV with her. She also liked to be greeted properly in the morning with "Good morning, Momma," not just "Good morning."

How absurd, I thought. I couldn't understand why these things were so upsetting to her. They seemed so trivial to me. I could understand the good morning, although I wasn't quite comfortable calling her Momma just yet. I barely knew her, and it felt odd to me to start calling her Momma, but I guessed I would try. But I still felt that it was unnecessary for me to sit with her the night before, especially since I felt stressed about organizing my room and getting ready for work the next morning. My job was quite stressful and it had been difficult to plan a wedding on top of having a demanding job. Now, my home life and dealing with my mother-in-law was going to be stressful too. Maybe I was overthinking it, but I did not feel her behavior was right. I wanted to discuss this with her, but had no idea how to approach her. She seemed very rigid in her ways, and I was starting to see that she ran the household with an iron fist. I was new here. I didn't know how I was going to find my place.

Over the next few months, I slowly adjusted to married life.

Adjusting to life with my husband, adjusting to living with his family, adjusting to living in a new city, adjusting to living in a new house;it felt overwhelming at times. Waking up each day, everything seemed so unfamiliar. As the weeks went by, it still didn't feel familiar or comfortable. We were given the master bedroom in the house, which I was grateful for. The room was large and spacious with lots of lights. There was a ravine behind our house with a lush forest filled with poplar and other types of deciduous trees. It was nice, I enjoyed the nature view from the bedroom.

But as soon as I would open the door of our bedroom and make my way downstairs, crippling anxiety would hit me. The tension in my head, down into my shoulders, down to my lower body. It felt debilitating.

As I entered the living room and kitchen part of the house, I always felt like I was walking on eggshells. I could feel the energy in the room; it was uncomfortable. I could feel myself hunch. My once-confident strides turned limp, and I would enter with my head down. The kitchen, along with the rest of the house, was kept spotless and minimalist. It was an uncomfortable clean, as if the house had no soul. There were four people living in this house, but if a stranger walked in, they would likely feel that no one lived here. She would spend at least three hours cleaning the house each day. She would wake up early at 5 a.m., do her prayers, and go downstairs at 6 a.m. to begin cleaning. She would cook as well, and then later, in the morning, she would go to work. I couldn't understand how she had all of this energy. She also stayed up late at night to watch TV. She barely ever slept. Even if she did sleep, she was a light sleeper who would wake up if my husband and I came home late. The opening of the garage door, walking up the stairs, one of which creaked, would be enough to wake her up in the late hours of the night.

Weekends were even worse. I would make my way down into the kitchen on a weekend, usually at 9 a.m., as I liked to sleep in during the weekends. She would be mopping the floor. Not an activity that I would want to do first thing in the morning. I remember looking around and thinking, what is even there to clean? She had literally cleaned the floors yesterday. I never said anything, though. The slow move into chaos would begin with me trying to cook for me and my husband. He liked what I made for breakfast, but, whenever I cooked, my then-brother-in-law would come in to turn the fan to full blast, because apparently he felt what I was cooking was stinky. His mom was vegetarian, which apparently made the rest of us criminals. Back at my parents' house, I used to love the smell of cooking, especially breakfast. How is cooking one egg smelling up the house? I could understand a curry dish, but one egg with little seasoning on it was enough to make the entire house smell?

After I would cook, I often received strange looks from both my mother-in-law and brother-in-law. As my mother-in-law did not eat eggs or meat, I never offered my food to her.

The day would descend into even more conflict and passive aggression where I would be told that I was not washing the dishes right or that there was a grain of rice on the floor—and while she would be rewashing the washed dishes, complaining about the grain, I would wonder how it had escaped her meticulous scrubbing. Wisely, I did not articulate these thoughts.

The evening would be spent watching TV—on her demand. We would all have to huddle and watch Indian soaps, whether we understood or related to any of it. I could swear I saw some of the sources for her strange ideas and ideals there too. It seemed to be her single biggest inspiration!

As if all this wasn't enough, the Punjabi Hindi debate was always on. My family was from Punjab and my parents and relatives all spoke Punjabi at home, so I was not used to being around Hindi speakers. My

Hindi was limited to Bollywood Hindi, which was different from the dialect my in-laws spoke at home. They spoke with a Bangalore accent to it. Often my mother-in-law, brother-in-law, and husband would have conversations in Hindi, with me also sitting there. I did not know what was going on, so I would tune out. Nobody noticed.

After an hour or so of watching annoying Indian TV, I would get up and usually give my husband a signal to either go to the basement and watch TV or to go to bed. He sometimes agreed, but mostly he would tell me to wait until Momma went to bed. I could see my mother-in-law give us a look, so I would stay longer. I felt that if she knew I wanted to leave the room and spend time alone with my husband, she would purposely stay up longer. Despite being tired and falling asleep on the couch, she would refuse to go upstairs and sleep until at least 11 p.m. I couldn't understand why she didn't value her sleep, knowing that she would be up at 5 a.m.

Every moment being around his family was painful. I began valuing my time at work more, this was the time I had to myself. When 4:30 p.m. would roll around, I would feel instant dread about going home.

About nine months into our marriage, I had changed jobs. I found a job closer to our house, which I would regret later. This new job cut my commute down to 15 minutes. On the one hand, I didn't have to wake up so early, but this also meant I was home before 5 p.m.—more time with the mother-in-law!

My brain began to think of creative ways to delay getting home. An extra hour at work suddenly didn't seem so bad. The fitness studio near work seemed even better. Especially the 5 p.m. class—perfection! A stroll in the mall or a meal by myself seemed more like hidden pleasures than the chore of being alone. I was not yet questioning why I seemed to enjoy being by myself and away from the house, even though I was married. And so, I was far, far away from questioning what I needed to do about it.

I had started drinking a lot more during this time; I felt a glass of wine or two calmed my nerves, and I was better able to deal with my home life. Other times, after work, I would aimlessly drive around the city and discover different areas, different parks and other interesting places. Somehow, the taste of fast food also made me feel better. At home, it was a bit harder to drink, but we did have a bar set up downstairs. My mother-in-law was against alcohol and did not allow us to keep any at home. But sometimes, I would secretly buy wine or vodka and sneak in a drink or two in the evenings, usually when my mother-in-law would step out of the house for a short bit. Sometimes, my husband and I would have a drink or two secretly downstairs, but often it was me alone. She had found out one time that we were consuming alcohol in the house, and she told my husband that he would never, ever, bring alcohol into the house again. So out of respect, he agreed. This was a loss to me, as I felt those times sitting together alone in the basement and enjoying wine together were some of our only special moments, just the two of us - and now that was being taken away from me too.

I felt like an underage teenager whose parents were keeping tabs on them. After a few weeks, I began to consume wine on my own at home. I was now secretly hiding it from my husband as well as my in-laws!

Over the next few months, things became progressively worse. The distance between him and I grew to an extent where it could easily accommodate tidal wave on tidal wave. The abyss was even deeper, and the thought of trying to bridge any of this was only exhausting. Did I even want to be competing for his attention? The one who chose his family over me? The one who wanted me to stay away from my own family?

Between his mother and brother pestering me, giving me unnecessary lectures about how joint families work and gender roles, and with my husband becoming more and more distant from me —I began feeling depressed. Thoughts of regret, leaving, even the D word began to enter my mind. Is this what our married life is supposed to be? Because if it is, then Indian women are being scammed and short-changed. This marriage setup seemed unfair and unjust.

Forget about losing my freedom and autonomy when it came to decisions for myself, I was not even consulted for decisions to do with our home or future. Every decision came after due consultation with his brother and mother.

I was an outsider in my own marriage.

If there was one point where I could pinpoint where my marriage hit rock bottom, it was at my brother-in-law's wedding. To this day, that wedding was the most dramatic wedding I have ever attended, and Indian weddings are usually full of drama! In fact, I have had nightmares about this wedding since, and on occasion I still do.

We had around 15 people total staying at the family home. With very little interest in the wedding but happiness to be meeting more of the family, I went along with the sister-in-law act. It was my close cousin's wedding, though, that sent me into a wave of isolation and sadness. I was missing all of that! While my family did their best to attend, I had too many responsibilities as the *Bahu Rani* to actually enjoy their company—or the wedding itself. Plus, their definition of a wedding and our definition of a wedding was very different. There was no joy here— only a "let's-get-this-over-with" attitude.

A strict, time-sensitive ceremony was the main event at the *Gurdwara*. I remember sitting nearby and watching the whole thing go by in a blur. My mother-in-law made it so clear how much she loved the new daughter-in-law's family—or maybe she just wanted to drive home a point and love-bomb the new victim. I would never know.

The *langar* followed in a tent outside, and I quietly sat eating my food. At this point, the bride's sisters had stolen the groom's shoes, my husband's shoes, and a few of their friends and cousins' shoes. I watched from my table as the sisters, the groom, and his boys negotiated the return of their shoes. The negotiation had been taking some time and the camera guys were filming the entire thing. One of my husband's cousins then approached me and said, "*Phabhi*, the girls took your car keys." He had driven me and some of our out of town guests in my car to the *Gurdwara*, as I did not want to drive in a punjabi suit, my husband drove with my brother-in-law in his vehicle. I suddenly felt so angry that these girls had taken my car keys as well, I felt it was going too far. I immediately got up and did not really think about what I was doing. I angrily rushed over to the bride's sister's and DEMANDED my car keys back.

In front of the 20–30 people gathered around the negotiation, in front of the cameras who had been filming, and all of my husband's extended family. I had just made a scene.

Perhaps it wasn't the car keys that set me off, but rather the warm reception this bride-to-be was getting from my in-laws. A degree of warmth and love I never felt from them. My mother-in-law had been more excited about this wedding than my own and couldn't stop from showing her enthusiasm, which started just days after my wedding. Instead of celebrating me as a new bride, welcoming me and loving me, they were constantly telling me how excited they were about the next daughter-in-law—younger, more religious, spoke better Punjabi—all things I was not.

My husband, with a very angry face, quickly rushed over to me and yelled at me to stop. He pulled me aside, and my mother-in-law was trying to calm me down. I immediately realized I made a big mistake.

At this point, there was a blur of phone calls being placed to my sister—to complain about me—and she was asked to talk some sense into me. I was asked to apologize to my husband. And the car keys made their way back to me. The sheer childishness of this situation came back to sting—as it had on many occasions when he had done the same thing during our fights.

To be fair, I was not sure what had triggered me. Maybe it was 10 months of trauma that had come bubbling to the surface, further amplified by the hordes of people and my mother-in-law's jabbing gaze.

Now I was to incur the wrath of the entire family. As if his brother and mother were not enough, his other relatives also began to talk about how I was not happy in this marriage. The gossip mill was churning big time! To state the obvious, I was in a miserable pit with no way out.

The rest of the wedding day, I kept breaking down and crying. One of my husband's aunts had to take me aside to calm me down. I didn't really partake in the rest of the day's activities, my husband and I barely spoke to each other the rest of the day. I knew he was angry at me, rightfully so. I still think that was one of the dumbest things I had ever done in my life. Sometimes we are the villain in our own marriage.

The very next day—the day of the reception—I was delivered an even more harsh judgment. When I came downstairs early that morning, my mother-in-law sat with my husband and I and expressed her disgust at how the wedding day went down. She looked right at me in the face and told me that my parents had taught me nothing.

No one asked me what I was going through. No one cared what I might be feeling. And they did not even seem to consider that they may have had something to do with this outburst. They were simply frustrated at it. Ironic. And very sad.

But I didn't want to cause any more drama, so I sat there silently while she continued on with her lecture.

As if that wasn't enough, at the evening's festivities, I was not even introduced by my dear husband, who was emceeing the event. The Bhua, Massi, Granddad—everyone got their due place in his speech. I was left out. There was visible disappointment radiating from the table where my parents sat, and openly questioning looks on why he hadn't mentioned my name.

As if all that wasn't enough, there was a small mishap on the dance floor where one of the nephews, in his exuberance, jammed his elbow in the bride's face and she had a bloodied nose. The chaos that ensued was deafening and mind-numbing. And yet again, my husband found a way to blame it all on me, even though I had finally managed to start enjoying the event a little bit.

He did not speak with me that day or the next.

After his brother's wedding, my marriage wasn't the same.

I was subject to even more passive aggression, escalated by the fact that the new people-pleasing *Devrani* now cast a long shadow over me. I could never win.

All I wanted was to be a priority for my husband, but all I got in return was constant tension. I wasn't the only one at the receiving end. My parents kept getting irate phone calls from my newly emboldened mother-in-law, who wanted to inform them that their parenting had failed the great Indian daughter-in-law test.

My parents became increasingly annoyed by these phone calls and didn't fully believe them either. Whenever I would see my mom, she would remind me to be good, be nice. My father told me to not say anything back to my husband or mother-in-law whenever they would say anything to me. It was hard to follow this advice.

The nagging about my work hours, not wearing the gold his family had given me, the amount of time I was spending with my family, it all only got worse. No one connected it with my husband's lack of understanding with me, and the fact that our lives had turned into a painful pile of rubble that I was quickly checking out.

On our first anniversary, instead of receiving the standard congratulatory greetings, my mother-in-law told me that I must change my personality. Change my personality and become a part of this family.

And then things took a turn for the worse.

They started keeping track of all my call logs in the hopes of finding something—anything—as evidence that I was a loose woman.

That storm came at me out of nowhere.

I found myself increasingly wondering if divorce was an option that I would have to turn to, and what it would even do for me. Around this point in time, I received a message from an old guy friend. When he inquired about my married life, I ended up telling him how miserable I was and what was happening. He actually suggested marriage counseling and it sparked a sudden interest in me to learn more about people's divorce journeys—just to see if there was light at the end of the tunnel. Very sweetly, this friend asked me to reach out anytime I wanted. In a six-month period, I called him about four or five times, mainly to talk about issues I was having in my marriage.

One Saturday, when I was at my parent's home because my husband was working, I decided to drive somewhere and spend some time by myself. I drove to a nearby industrial area, instead of going straight home. As I parked the car, I got a call from my husband—it had been no more than 20 minutes. He wanted to know where I was since he had called my parents, and they said I had left home a while ago. My entire existence felt the suffocation coming through in that question and what my life had become.

When I told him I was on my way home, he screamed at me, asking what I was doing at the industrial park! I realized at that moment that I was being tracked. I did not know how, but I knew there was a tracker somewhere.

That night was the last night we spent together at that house.

We had argued and argued for hours that night before we eventually went to bed. He had informed my parents what happened and in the morning he was going to take me back to my parents house. The next morning, we got up and barely spoke. He was going to take his car, and I was going to take my car. I packed a few of my clothes as I knew that I would be going back to my parents home for a few days. I didn't know that it would be permanent.

Later that week, we decided to meet in a coffee shop. We talked for a couple of hours, and I tried to tell him everything that was bothering me, but it would make him angry. He would then turn things around at me, and at one point we found ourselves yelling at each other in the Starbucks.

He then came over to my parents' house at the end of the week and decided that he would sleep over. He was acting quite nice, as if nothing had happened, and was being very affectionate towards me. The next morning, he pulled out his laptop and asked me for my cell phone login. I wasn't quite sure what he was trying to do, but I didn't think much of it and gave him my login and password. He logged in and immediately started going through my call logs. He was digging for information.

He came back to my parents' house in the evening, and we went to the basement to talk. He pulled out an envelope with a stack of paper. He had printed all of my call logs, going back six months. He had highlighted a couple phone calls. He asked me who this phone number belonged to, as I had spoken to this person quite recently around two or three times for around 15 minutes each. My heart sank—I hadn't told him that I had spoken to this friend. He wasn't someone I hung out with regularly, I had not met him at all during our marriage, and we didn't have anything going on between us. I hadn't thought it was something I should have told him.

He went through my phone and discovered his name. He asked me who he was, and I told him he was an old friend. Why are you talking to another guy? he screamed at me. I pleaded with him, telling him that he was just an old friend I had known for years and nothing was going on between us. In his anger he left, and I was at a loss.

Suddenly I got a strange WhatsApp message on my phone, it was in our family group with my in-laws. My brother-in-law shared a photo of my friend in the group! It was a photo of him he had found on social media, asking if this was the guy. I realized that this was going to blow up and I had no control.

How had something so innocent turned into such a massive attack on my character? I was only talking to a friend—and that too about things that my husband did not understand. Perhaps I was wrong, but even if this had been a female friend, I would have been discussing the same things with her.

My parents were trying their best to keep my mind off the situation. I had spent almost a week with them. I had tried to contact my husband, but he wasn't responding much to my calls or texts. He had gone quiet. My parents advised me to let him cool down. He had anger issues and did not know how to process his emotions. It had always been difficult for me to express my feelings to him, as he would get angry when I told him I don't feel good or comfortable. Perhaps that's why I began to hide my feelings from him, perhaps that's why I was expressing my feelings to everyone but him. My mother, my sister, my friends, even a male friend.

Then things got to a point where there was no turning around.

It all happened in a blur. The doorbell rang and standing outside were my husband, his brother, his mother, his *massi ji* and *fuffar ji*. Before we could make sense of what was happening, they were standing in our living room with utter disregard for the fact that they had shown up unannounced at an inconvenient hour.

My husband and I were both silent during the entire meeting. I remember my brother-in-law trying to make himself look important leading the conversation, talking over anyone who tried to say anything. At one point, it turned into a shooting match between him and my mother. This wasn't a meeting but an ambush.

My mother tried her best to defend me. "Our daughter was born in Canada." She said, adding that he was born in India and the culture was different. This angered both his brother and mother. My mother-in-law screamed at my mother. My brother-in-law and mother-in-law were hellbent on airing out their grievances and did not come for a productive conversation. They wanted to show that I was a terrible daughter-in-law and sister-in-law. What would be the point of reconciling now? They had shown their true colors in every way. Even if we were to reconcile, his family would always think badly of me.

After they left, my dad turned to me. I thought he would be angry, I thought I let him down. But to my amazement, he asked me in the most loving way if I was okay. I was shaking at this point, he held me close to him and told me, "*Beta*, don't worry. You are safe here, you don't need to go back to them."

This was profound.

Indian fathers don't usually vouch for their daughters, particularly if their marriage has failed. But my father never let anyone say anything to me after my separation. My dad was angry at my ex, and particularly angry at his brother and mother. He expressed that the brother had no right to speak to me and my family in that way and didn't have the right to make decisions or influence my marriage.

Both of my siblings were getting married a few months after my separation. It was the worst timing, but I had to make the most of it. Leading up to the weddings, I was trying my best to make up with my ex so that he could attend the weddings. I wanted to save face and not embarrass my family in front of my relatives. I didn't know how they would react to me being separated. My parents also had not given the news of my separation to any of our relatives. My parents had actually gone to my in-law's house and personally delivered an invitation for my sister's wedding.

The week of my sister's wedding came, and still I had not been able to reconcile with my ex. Her wedding was beautiful, but my ex never showed up. I was disappointed and hurt. A couple of my relatives had asked where he was, and I gave them some excuse that he was busy with a family emergency.

Six weeks later was my brother's wedding. I had given my ex an invitation, but at this point I knew he was not going to attend. My brother's wedding week came and went without any drama. My ex didn't attend and this time, none of my relatives even asked where my husband was. It was a relief. I guess people had figured it out on their own.

As the months went by, more and more people found out about my separation. I also began to talk about it. Talking helped. I found that, contrary to my initial thoughts, everyone was supportive. No one told me to go and reconcile with him just for the sake of staying married. All of my relatives, including the most "Desi" of my relatives, were supportive and told me that I should do whatever is best for me and my happiness.

Although my marriage did not go the way I wanted, I believe that no amount of catering to in-laws and even a man is worth giving up one's own mental sanity. The constant judgment, scrutiny and passive aggressive comments and behavior is enough to emotionally damage anyone.

I often go back in time and recall the "gift" that my ex's mother had deemed fit to give me on our first wedding anniversary.

Early that morning, she started her speech. No "happy anniversary," no "congratulations."

She said, "Today on your first anniversary, here's what I want you to learn and know. You have a very long way to go in terms of learning how to become a part of a family and dedicating yourself to them. Today, I am giving you a crucial lesson and feedback. You have not been able to fit in properly or be a good daughter-in-law. You must try harder to learn and be a better fit for this family."

I should have realized then that I didn't need to be in that marriage. But now, I hope Desi women learn this for themselves and to start questioning lines and speeches like these.

Marriage might be a beautiful destination, but it is not the only one. And the cost of the ticket should not be your identity, your mental health, or an unaccountable partner who holds you accountable for everything.

I realized that after this experience, marriage is not the be all and end all accomplishment that our Desi society heavily encourages. Many of us don't fit into the mold of a perfect Indian *bahu* and that is perfectly ok. We as women have the freedom to pursue our own passions and interests, and if we do choose to get married, we should do it on our own terms, not on our in-laws.

Now, I am healing—and more than myself, I am healing the values inside me that are not helpful for me or any other Desi girl. I am traveling and living life on my own terms.

Sabrina Kaur works in the corporate world and lives in Vancouver, Canada. Since turning 40, she has made the decision to prioritize self-care. She has traveled to nine countries and hopes to travel to as many as possible before turning 50. Travel was something she didn't get to do in her 20s and 30s, so she is making it up in her 40s. She has a strong sense of breaking free from the traditional Indian girl role and carving a unique path for herself. She believes Desiwomen should not limit themselves to who they date or marry, or even not marry at all. She is open to connecting with like-minded women or anyone who needs guidance in living for themselves and not for others.

THE DESI DIVORCEE

Springing to Life

NOOPURA HUDDAR

It was a beautiful spring day. The magnolias were blooming outside my local courthouse.

We took our vows under the full, pink tree, with only the judge in attendance to officiate and witness our wedding. A passerby cheered us on as he drove past us.

It was just days before the COVID-19 pandemic was starting to take hold of the world.

My family and relatives joined us for a ceremony over a video call after we got back from the courthouse. My mom said nothing during the call. She was happy that I was getting married and approved of my husband. I'm not sure what made her stay silent through the call.

Everyone accepted the small, virtual ceremony on the condition that we would travel to India as soon as possible for a "real" wedding.

A few months earlier, when I was in India shopping for my engagement ceremony with my parents, my mom and I fought about the dress I wanted to buy.

"It's so expensive!" she said, "Why do you need to spend so much on something you're going to wear once?!" I thought about the piles of extravagant sarees she had collected over the years but hardly ever wore, and I wanted no part in the stress and arguments of the inevitable wedding if this was the kind of friction a small engagement was going to cause.

Many women grow up dreaming about their wedding day—the venue, the food, the outfits. But the heavy clothes and jewelry, the spending, strangers swarming all around you, the constant fighting as everyone tried to get their wishes met, and the show of it all—I didn't care for any of it. For a day that should be a celebration of a union, it seems to only cater to everyone's enjoyment but the couple's.

Seeing the expectations placed on women in Indian marriages made me not want it for myself. Marriage looked like a continuous compromise on the woman's part, with no promise of fulfillment. Still, I grew up hearing about my family's plans for my wedding—and everyone had their own ideas of what the big, fat affair would be like. I thought my destiny was set.

Thankfully, it never came to pass.

My partner and I never traveled to India together again, and I got a divorce before COVID-19 was no longer considered a pandemic.

The day I turned 23, my parents turned up the pressure to get married. "Happy birthday!" They said, "We're going to start looking for a husband for you now."

I'd always been rebellious, and found it hard to fall in line with expectations that family and society had of me. There was a lot of internal friction with the idea of an arranged marriage; the entire concept sounded so icky to me. But in this collectivistic society, individual desires are not as valued as the needs of the whole.

Even though I wasn't ready to go through an arranged marriage, and preferred to find a partner myself, I had not defined for myself what a good marriage could look like. My thoughts on marriage were so heavily influenced by my family that I couldn't move beyond them to understand healthy partnerships and what it would take to get there.

When I started dating, I had an idea of what I wanted, but I didn't have a good grasp on how to screen for the qualities I wanted in a partner, and how deceptive some personalities can initially be.

My parents' marriage was traditional and arranged. I don't know many details of the matchmaking process, but I can hazard a guess that they didn't meet more than a few times before they were wed. My mother continued to work after marriage, and often alluded to stories of handling housework, a career, and children, while being a good wife and daughter-in-law.

Their marriage is far from healthy.

So the idea of picking a life partner from a pool of people based on a biodata—essentially your life resume—seemed entirely superficial. It didn't consider any aspects of compatibility, such as temperament, conflict resolution skills, emotional maturity, an ability to be there for you, or anything, really, that actually matters in a life partner.

I imagined what my biodata would look like amongst the pool of tall, slim, fair-skinned women who didn't wear glasses and were "family-oriented."

Weight: 57kg
Height: 5 ft.
Complexion: Dusky
Manglik: No
Eyeglasses: Yes
The focus was on your looks, your height, skin color, weight, whether you wore glasses, your education level, workplace, salary, how adjusting and accommodating you were and, of course, your family's reputation. These were deemed as being important considerations in a relationship, as opposed to softer qualities like emotional maturity, compassion, and kindness.

Looking back, it's so obvious I was surrounded by narcissism in my family before I met my ex-husband. It appeared in several forms growing up, a lot of which showed up as belittling and being raised to cater to everyone else's demands. The way my family interacted with one another was disguised as intense love and care. This made it all the more confusing to separate the two when it came to romantic relationships. And since I was brought up as a people pleaser—heavily rewarded for being a good girl and punished for speaking up for myself—going against my desires made sense. I fell into a toxic relationship—one in which I felt I had little to no agency, but I believed it was the best I could get.

So many women do not realize how much their parents influence their choice of partner. In my case, my upbringing with narcissistic parents allowed me to normalize a narcissistic partner.

The biggest red flags were not in my ex-husband; they were in the way I had been parented and what I was taught to value—women being rewarded for being "good" wives and not standing up for themselves at home.

How did I meet and choose this red flag, though?

I met my ex-husband, let's call him Al, through Bumble. It was August 2019, and he was a student at Purdue University. I had already graduated from the same university with a master's degree but continued to work in the same town. I remember thinking he was cute, and being really excited to go on a date with him. He seemed easy to talk to, so I wasn't particularly nervous.

"He's really wonderful, I can't allow myself to take him for granted," I remember thinking to myself. This was a time in my life where I was focused on personal growth—thinking positively, and showing gratitude. I swung to the extreme, forcing myself to show gratitude for things that may have felt slightly off in my body.

I had a history of ending relationships at the six-month mark or thereabouts, and instead of realizing that I was good at getting out of situations that didn't work for me, I saw it as something to work on, put more effort into.

We connected quickly over the next few months. He seemed almost perfect—charming and smart, good-looking, self-assured, *and* very interested in me, which made me feel special. It all felt new and exciting. I felt like I was chasing him, but I wanted to be around him more as time went by. It started to feel like I was keener on moving things forward, and like I had to drag him along on the journey.

Something felt off, but I didn't know what it was. There were inconsistencies in his actions and words, but I'd grown up in a similar environment where this was very normalized. You simply didn't call people out on their behavior, on how they treated you, or hold them to any standard. It didn't feel quite right, but also not wrong enough to seriously question things. Sometimes, it feels safer to stay in an unhappy but familiar place, rather than risk losing what you have. This was very true for me, because I didn't have good relationship role models growing up, and had no reference for what I could aspire to have in a relationship.

There wasn't a strong reason to end it, so the only option that made sense was to move forward.

"Why don't you move in?" I asked after a few months. We were at each other's places all the time, so it seemed like the logical next step. He hemmed and hawed and eventually brought some of his stuff over.

Living with him was like living with a teenage boy who wanted me to be his mother. He expected me to do the chores, cook for him, clean up after him, help him with his classes, and of course, please him sexually whenever he was in the mood, which was all the time.

There's nothing more antithetical to being someone's romantic and sexual partner than having to be their mother. True to his narcissistic tendencies, I came to see just how performative the sex was—focused on his pleasure—manipulative, coercive, and lacking any respect for me or my boundaries.

There was a complete lack of integrity and accountability with Al. He was good at saying what needed to be said during conflict (in order to get past it) but it ended there. There was no followthrough; the expectation was that I would learn to deal with things the way they were. Any attempts at bringing up my concerns were met with deflection and stonewalling; I was the problem for not letting things go.

Still, I continued in the relationship. I had no idea at the time how wrong this was, and the lasting effects it would have on my mental health. I thought that this was just how things were, and tried to focus on the positives.

But this wasn't just an internal voice.

"As long as the positives are there, it's all good and you should proceed. No relationship is perfect."

I decided to talk to a family friend, a marriage and family counselor. This was her professional opinion. Her views were influenced by South Asian culture, and echoed ideas around marriage and partnership that I had learned growing up. Several friends and relatives said similar things. I was trying to validate my feelings through other people because I'd been unable to validate my own feelings and experiences. When I got this advice, I chose to dismiss my intuition, and continued to stay in this relationship.

I gave up my power.

In December 2019, I had planned a trip home to India. I knew I wouldn't go back for a few years after this, so, Al and I decided we would travel together to meet my family. We were already on the path to marriage at that point, so I decided to break the news to my parents.

"Your daughter has found us a son-in-law!!" my mom urgently yelled through the bathroom door to my dad. This was the reaction I expected the moment I told her I was seeing someone. We set up a video call so that my parents would get a chance to talk to Al before we went to India. There was no actual proposal, just a conversation for him to understand what it meant for our future if he decided to go to India with me.

There were a couple of things that happened around the trip that reinforced Al's irresponsible nature and complete lack of accountability. I was already in India for a week before he would come meet me there. Right as he was leaving my apartment, he messaged to say the main door knob came off. He proceeded to the airport without updating me on what he did to fix it before he left the country, if he did anything at all. When we got back from India, I found that the stove was on. Al was super paranoid, scanning the rooms because he was convinced someone had broken in. Someone who didn't take anything but left the stove on, of all things? In both situations, he showed no contrition, and took no accountability.

Of course, the family adored him, and fawned over him the entire time he was there. He was good-looking, smart, and on his way to becoming an engineer. That was all they needed.

I still had my doubts about him and marriage in general, but the pressure from my family pushed me into agreeing to a last-minute engagement ceremony before we traveled back to the US. I agreed—I thought it was an inevitable outcome at this point since my family had already met him, and I went along with it with the feeling of wanting to rip the Band-Aid off.

We got back right before the pandemic hit. Within a month of being back, my workplace conducted layoffs. I lost my job and, with it, my chance of being picked in the H-1B lottery, which was my only path to continuing to live and work in the country without getting married. This hadn't been outside the realm of possibility, so I had applied for, and received, Canadian permanent residency a year ago. I didn't have many options, but moving back home—back to a toxic environment I'd spent years trying to escape—was not one I was willing to consider.

Al was adamant about not moving to Canada, which was understandable since he was still enrolled in college and working on his undergraduate degree. What puzzled me was his refusal to even entertain the idea of me moving there temporarily, so I could work while we figured out our future together.

"I'm not going to be your weekend husband," he declared, when I suggested I at least look for jobs outside of the immediate vicinity. It had taken me a good 10 months, and thousands of applications to get a job after I graduated, and this was an even more dire situation. He didn't understand how difficult it was to get a job as an immigrant, especially one who only had one more shot at an H-1B, and a very small timeframe in which to do it. He was, however, very comfortable deciding if and where I could look for a job, confidently assuring me that I could get a job nearby as time continued to run out.

My work permit expired soon after, and I ran out of time to look for jobs in the US. Moving to Canada did not seem like an option anymore, thanks to Al's reaction. I felt like I couldn't leave without ending the relationship and breaking off the engagement, which I wasn't brave enough to do at the time.

"So when is the wedding?" my dad asked without skipping a beat, when I called to tell my parents about parts of the situation. It seemed like an obvious next step to them, the clear solution to the problem at hand. Their reaction only reinforced the nightmare I felt stuck in—a room with no doors except the one that led to marriage, to a person I wasn't sure was right for me. The only way I could avoid moving back home was getting married, but to somebody who never made me feel like I was at home either.

Everyone's desires overrode my internal dialogue, and in trying to escape a different situation, I let myself be pushed into a decision from a place of fear, instead of a wholeness and assurance that this would be good for my future.

The 1998 movie *Sliding Doors*, starring Gwyneth Paltrow as Helen Quilley, explored two alternate storylines based on two different paths Helen's life could have taken, depending on whether or not she caught a train.

The decision to proceed with the wedding closed the door on what could possibly have been a very different life. I often wonder where I would be today if I had made different choices then, but I don't dwell on it too much. Even so, it never sat right with me when people said, "I wouldn't change a thing because it got me to where I am today." There's an underlying assumption there that I don't agree with. As it stands, I did the best I could with what I knew, and that's enough.

"Tutel titka tanu nakos," my mom said when I hinted to her that things were not good between Al and me after our marriage. Loosely translated, it means, "Don't stretch things so far that they break." The message was clear—you may be unhappy, but figure out a way to compromise and make it work, because keeping the marriage intact is paramount.

I knew this of course, but that was when I realized again that I could not turn to my parents for support. They may have had good intentions, but their intentions were heavily influenced by what people would say if they found out I was divorced.

Things got worse with time. I tried talking to Al, to bring up my concerns and my desires. He was completely uninterested in hearing what I wanted from a partner, and a marriage. He was convinced I would never leave, that he had free rein to do whatever he liked without consequence.

No one really understood what I was dealing with, especially not family. Al seemed to have no empathy, and lacked any inclination to form a genuine, meaningful connection with me or understand my point of view. His strong narcissistic tendencies became an impossibly large hurdle.

It had an outsized impact, not just on the relationship, but also my mental health. There was constant gaslighting, blame, and deflection. A lack of followthrough, accountability, or responsibility. Entitlement and hidden agendas. I was lost in this web of confusion, and started questioning my own reality. I felt like I couldn't build the relationship I wanted with Al, no matter how much effort I put into it.

I would have found it hard to believe this about someone had I not experienced it for myself. So, though I could see why my parents had a hard time with it, their lack of support and an inability to believe my version of events still hurt. I grieved the loss of the relationship I had dreamed of building, and the loss of a family system that could emotionally support me.

Al had an addictive personality and was paranoid by nature. These tendencies, which he leaned into, were exacerbated by PTSD from his experiences in the military. He consistently relied on substance use to *have fun,* even when it wasn't in a social setting. Alcohol and weed were always front and center in his mind, in a way that I never was. He was constantly looking for opportunities to indulge, even though it made his paranoia worse.

Election season began soon after COVID-19. With classes moving online, Al was free to indulge, and soon developed a strong paranoia about the government. He spent most of that summer and fall in contact with various small-scale extremist groups, even though he would never describe them as such. This continued for months—anonymous email and chat apps to ensure his identity was hidden, and using code names to refer to himself and other people, should their communication be intercepted by the authorities.

Al was also a staunch supporter of the Second Amendment, and kept a rifle in the trunk of his car and a pistol on him at most times. He would carry it with him to go to the store, or even out to a restaurant. I expressed my discomfort about this several times, but his convictions were too strong to be shaken by my discomfort.

What may have started as a genuine attempt at enacting change in the political system, soon seemed to turn into extremism. He described various not-so-legal things that the groups he was part of were thinking of doing, like damaging public property.

When this caught the attention of a national law agency, it led to an investigation that lasted over two years. He narrowly escaped arrest, lost his security clearance, but kept his spot in school. He admitted no wrongdoing, and refused to consider the implications of his actions on his wife's life.

Things continued to deteriorate between us. He didn't change his behavior at all, only looked for smarter ways to continue doing what he was doing without being caught.

I, in turn, turned to alcohol and weed to numb myself and slow the constant churn of thoughts in my head. It was my only escape. This self-abandonment pushed me further down the spiral of deteriorating mental health. I hated sleeping in the same bed as him.

I didn't want to feel this way anymore. I decided, again, to open myself up to my husband, the person who promised to take care of me in sickness and in health. I admitted to him, I had been having suicidal thoughts.

"I'll never allow someone to manipulate me like that again," he declared, as he walked away. How was I manipulating him? Why didn't he care that I was struggling? Who could I turn to in the depths of my despair, if not him?

I felt powerless. By now I was suffering from severe anxiety, and slid into severe depression. I could not live with the cognitive dissonance. How could I—someone who had accomplished so much in life and overcome so many hurdles—allow someone to treat me like this?

I began googling his behavior, and things finally fell into place. I found a name for what I was experiencing—Narcissistic Personality Disorder.

It was empowering to learn that the issue wasn't with how I was communicating, or how hard I was trying. I binge-watched and listened to every single video and podcast I could find about NPD, and realized that the relationship was unlikely to change or get better with time. Narcissistic personalities are rooted in a lack of awareness about the self and a lack of empathy for others—the perfect recipe for not making any changes to the status quo.

I wanted to take some space, be by myself, and calm my mind to think through everything I had learned and experienced. But there were practical issues to work through—I was still unemployed, without an income of my own, and savings that had been depleted over the past several months of unemployment. After a lot of deliberation, I contacted a local women's shelter. They never got back to me.

I felt stuck. Except I wasn't.

I just wasn't ready to admit it to myself yet.

"In the depths of winter, I finally learned that within me there lay an invincible summer."

– Albert Camus, Lyrical and Critical Essays

What I needed was a divorce.

I had hit rock bottom, turned into a version of myself I could hardly recognize. I had fiercely worked my entire life to be independent and live on my own terms, and here I was—financially dependent on someone who thought he could dictate how I lived my life, a "partner" who didn't truly care about me or my well-being.

'What will people think?' echoed through my head, but there was a lot more than that holding me back. Remaining in the U.S. was tied to my marriage. I had applied for and gotten a conditional green card almost a year into my marriage, but I could only apply to remove the conditions on it after two years, provided I was still married and living with my husband then.

I was stuck between a rock and a hard place. My choices were either to stay in an unhappy marriage, or give up the life I'd built here over the last seven years, move to a new country, and start over. I resented my husband's privilege; a divorce would hardly even register as a blip in his life. His family would be on his side, and there would be no consequences for his life or work. He understood very well how a divorce would disrupt my life, which is why he thought I wouldn't actually leave, no matter what happened.

From the moment we got engaged, Al had started joking about how he had "trapped" me and how I couldn't leave him. He started pushing me to have kids the day after we got married, something that would have made it even harder for me to leave the marriage. But I stood my ground—I was not going to consider this prospect until I felt like we were a solid team, and that he was willing to be a hands-on and engaged parent. And we were so far away from that.

Children do not fix bad marriages.

My mom urged me to stick it out until the conditions on my green card were removed. She believed it was worth it to stay for however long it took; I could not imagine staying another minute. Nothing was worth losing my mental and physical health. Uncertainty breeds anxiety, and uncertainty about my future, my life, led to crippling anxiety. I had to do something, I decided. I tried to focus on things within my control, and worry less about the unknowns. Worrying helped me prepare to an extent, but it lost its utility fast.

*"Inaction breeds doubt and fear. Action
breeds confidence and courage."*

- Dale Carnegie

Making decisions and taking action set me free. I slowly got my sense of agency back, and I stopped feeling powerless.

What must die for you to be able to truly live?

I realized that I had to take decisive action to set myself free. I slowly got my sense of agency back and stopped feeling powerless. I learned that in order to live for myself, I had to let a part of my life and my old identity die.

The part that was trying to live up to my parents' expectations. The part of trying to be the obedient daughter who did not stray from the traditional path—marriage, a house, kids—because I owed them something. The part that lived for their approval and by their rules. All these parts had to die a spectacular death for me to discover myself and start living a life that aligned with me. The journey started inside me.

I had been too scared to break off the engagement, but I had to face my worst fears and get a divorce.

This meant coming to terms with them potentially disowning me, or, at the very least, having a very strained relationship from that point on. It meant that I might have to leave the country, start a new life in a new place, and find new work and community for myself wherever I ended up.

Getting a divorce veered me so off course from the path they saw for me, that I truly felt free to set off on my own path from that point on.

I built a new identity for myself—one that was not centered on meeting the needs of others. I had done that in some ways over the years, but always within the confines of being a good child. Getting a divorce was a rebirth for me, an opportunity to dismantle and discard everything I'd taken on from the outside world and really look within.

I refused to take on the shame and guilt people tried to hand me. I knew what I'd been through, and I was proud of the steps I'd taken to move into this new life. If people wanted to judge me for taking care of myself, so be it. If they wanted to keep it under wraps and not openly tell people that I was divorced, that was their choice.

I was lucky to have geographical separation from my family. While they continued to stay quiet about the divorce with family and friends, I was able to continue living life on my own terms on the other side of the world.

My divorce has not, and will never, define me. I refuse to let guilt become a part of my identity. I emerged on the other side of my divorce a completely different person—stronger, wiser, more resilient. I discarded the beliefs that society tried to force upon me, and became someone who did not look for validation outside of herself. Someone who could be vulnerable with the right people, and who had the strength to walk away from people who didn't deserve that vulnerability. Someone who knows her worth and will not settle for anything less than she deserves.

Someone who can bloom wherever she's planted.

Noopura Huddar grew up in Pune, India and moved to the US in 2015 to pursue a career in mechanical and aerospace engineering.

Noopura's mission is to curate conversations and stories about navigating separation and divorce in the South Asian community through her new podcast, Chai and Change, to help women navigate the complexities of separation and divorce by finding strength and resilience within themselves.

Noopura lives in Florida with her two adorable cats, Wubbo and Smudge. You can contact Noopura at noopura.huddar@gmail.com.

Follow Noopura's podcast on Instagram: @chaiandchangepodcast

Un-Shutting Up

MISRIYA JACKSI

After Divorce

Nothing I'm about to share with you is black or white. There are no villains or heroes in my story, it is more a story of a girl, finally coming into her own. We each come "into our own" in different ways/stages. This is part of my journey.

What humbled me on this journey was learning how to share my unfiltered thoughts with softness in the right settings. Not trauma dumping, or relying too heavily on my family/friends to be there for me emotionally at all times. I have learned how to give my loved one's space and grace after noticing my own unhealthy habits and coping mechanisms. I learned to forgive myself and others.

This journey has been *so* joyful. Full of beautiful moments. And some challenging ones too, which proved to be great teachers. Perhaps the individual who hurt me the most is *myself* in all this. Perhaps the biggest lesson that this has taught me is to view others through a lens of love. This journey was like a big boomerang and that brought me to a wonderful place where I could once again, drop the victim mentality, accept responsibility for my role as a soul on this earth, that strives to embody love in this life.

Even the hardest day after my divorce was better than my easiest day as a married woman.

Why? Because as a divorcee, I finally had the agency to make my own choices: the freedom to make choices after three decades of others making them for me. This freedom came with its own lessons—and I embraced them heartily, sometimes after a pause to reflect.

One of the first lessons I learned on my newfound journey was the freedom to make decisions, and take responsibility for those decisions.

I'm happy to report, from the other side, that this journey has been completely worth it. *Now I have the freedom to speak my mind freely, unfiltered.*

Anyway, enough reflections for now. Let's start this story from the start:

During Marriage

Getting married is something I dreamed about since I was a little girl. But not in the normal vanilla way. I genuinely thought my husband would love me like Raj from *Dilwale Dulhania Le Jaenge*, I'd be all happy like Madhuri from the first half of *Hum Aap Ke Hain Kaun*, and when we married, it would just be a way better version of *Hum Saath Saath Hai*.

And boy, were my prayers answered for that last part. I definitely felt like I stepped into my *Hum Saath Saath Hai* future when I got married in 2014 in Tanzania to a man who was son number three of four in a joint family household. I was the newest member of the family, the 12th person living in that home of four generations; ten adults, two children, the youngest of whom was 40 days old. The entire family was extremely kind, warm, and welcoming.

I was ecstatic. Overjoyed. Wow, my dreams came true. I lived in Dar es Salaam, Tanzania, my birthplace, again, after being away for over a decade. My home, where my soul was at peace, and where the beach and the ocean were in our backyard. My husband was a kind man, we were in love, we had great banter and laughed together all the time. He was never rude or mean to me, and was a great listener. Unlike many males I had seen who were not kind to their wives, he was kind to me and those around him. He was humble, even though he could have chosen to be egotistical. Unlike many families I had seen in my world, this family didn't restrict me from working, or having a business, or traveling for work. They really supported my career goals. I truly felt freer and more empowered in this new life as a wife than in my childhood home, which had so many rules. Here there were rules too, but on many other levels, I had freedom.

It was a big deal to be a grown woman building a family, with a career on the side. I wanted to be married, and I was finally married. I was finally out of my house.

Before Marriage/Childhood

Growing up in Dar es Salaam as a third generation Desi was *magical*. Our family left South Asia when there was no India and Pakistan, it was "Hindustan". There is a massive Desi diaspora in East Africa and all over Africa. My family is from Zanzibar Island and Tanga Town in Tanzania, so we are very Tanzanian and also very Desi. We speak Kiswahili, as well as Hindi, Urdu, Gujarati, and Kutchi. Most of the Desis who are in Tanzania culturally and linguistically connect with both Tanzania and South Asia. I grew up in a very large, fun-loving extended family. Family dinners, picnics, going away for the weekend to the beach were all a norm in my family. I had 26 cousins by the time I was 13, and life was a *blast*. And although I grew up in a community where singing, dancing, music and films were forbidden, my family was totally a lover of the arts. Yes, they practiced the religion and participated in culture, however when it was just us at home or during picnics, we would sing, dance, play sports, crack jokes amongst each other, elders, and young'uns, women and men, it didn't matter—we were all family. There was no hierarchy (unlike with my ex-in-laws once I got married) and it was so much fun.

In my life, I used to have a lot of fun with my family, but I also faced resistance in a household I considered "too strict." It was along the lines of, "Be independent and focus on school, but leave your opinions at the door and be a *daayi chokri* (good girl) at home." Basically, be perfectly domesticated, and perfectly social at the same time. Trained to be the perfect *daayi chokri*.

I was considered "too emotional" in my family. I used to look to my friends and community to support me when going through difficult moments. My family had a great ability to move on as if nothing happened, even if a lot happened. This was a great thing most times, but sometimes, I felt like important things were not being addressed, and that really irked me. I love my family, no family is perfect—but I never knew how to navigate this aspect. I didn't learn how to properly emotionally regulate myself until very recently, when some friends shared some tough love with me. I didn't even have awareness of what I would put my loved ones through when I was triggered in some situations. I wasn't dealing with my triggers in healthy ways. So many of them stemmed from my experiences of sexual abuse at a young age. I have learned a lot since then, more on this later.

Divorce /After Divorce

When I told my parents about my divorce, they were very supportive and positive; they even helped me secure a place to live. I'm so grateful for their open minds and support. The flip side of taking it so positively is that they never understood the emotional impact of going through a breakup like that. I don't blame them, though. They met one another when they were very young, married each other, and had stayed married. Their experiences and choices were so different from mine, how could I expect them to understand? That didn't mean they didn't want what was best for us. They dedicated so much of their lives to us. They took such good care of us. I am so grateful. These things are layered.

When I look back, although there was a lot of joy in each stage of life, there came with it as well a lot of pretense, partially because of certain social environments to which I was exposed. There were many pressures on women to keep the family together; for me, this looked like resolving conflicts at home before marriage, putting a stop to gossip at home after marriage, and defusing tension as much as possible. I lived in large families both before and after marriage and, honestly, neither of my homes were perfect. As my sister-in-law lovingly explained to me once:

Neither of our homes are perfect, no human or relationship is perfect either. So true.

Having said that, within imperfect relationships, the ability to speak freely – and be allowed to contribute to the environment and decisions in the home *matters*. It really felt like – both before and after marriage – I always had to march to the beat of someone else's drum – with absolutely no reasonable amount of agency or space to provide input. Is it the fault of those around me? Doesn't matter. I knew that it was my responsibility to create a space for myself to be able to have a say—if that's what I truly desired. And that's where my divorce journey began. It's not just that I divorced my husband. I divorced my old way of life, my old self. It was a rebirth. I gave birth to our son Hassan, and he birthed me too.

I realize now that on some level, I also got married to get more freedom than I had at home. Culturally the way I was raised, your world opens up only after you get married, not before. For example, I loved wearing sarees, but I was told this can only happen after marriage. I wanted to be a married woman so I could build my own life with my own rules, not march to the beat of someone else's drum forevermore. That didn't work out when I did get married, so now do I punish my ex and his family for that forever? Or torture myself by forcing myself to be someone I know I am not for his sake? Or simply let him go and create the space to be me and for him to be himself separately? Where we are not causing or taking upon ourselves more chaos than we need to.

"Jab We Met" - (Before Marriage)

It was never this complicated when my ex and I met. We had the most adorable meet-cute. We met when we were out with mutual friends, one of whom was my cousin. In true *"Dar"* fashion, we all went to the local shisha hotspot. It was all the rage back in 2013. There was a short time span during that outing when my ex and I were alone at the table, we exchanged really healthy banter and laughter. I didn't think much of it. When we were heading out, all five of us got trapped in the elevator together. It was hilarious. Electricity was gone. So we were stuck for a while until they got the power back. We were all laughing and cracking jokes in the elevator. The power came on but that moment in the elevator would stay with me forever. When I got home that night, I was still laughing from all that happened when I got a text from my cousin asking if he could send my number to his friend, my ex. We started communicating, and had two amazing dates before I had to fly back to Toronto. By the time I landed, I had a text from him. It said: "I told my mom about you." I looked at my phone and smiled. I was like what? That quickly? Soon after, they sent an official proposal and it was decided. We were to be engaged two months after our first meeting, and married 6 months after our engagement. It was quick, we were in love.

And we stayed in love the entire time. Only the last year of our marriage was challenging. In retrospect, I realize I could have handled some things better, as could those around me. After the loss of our son, we went to therapy and realized we wanted entirely different lives. We let each other go in peace instead of forcing one of us to have to completely compromise on vital future choices. Regardless of my ex and I having an eventual expiry date, I'm so grateful for each and every single moment and connection as a result of this marriage. I don't regret having this experience at all. It was a beautiful one. It was only after close to 7 years of being married, our son's passing and therapy thereafter did we realize we may not be best suited for one another. But we gave it a valiant effort. And we enjoyed it. I read a stat that said 80 percent of couples that lose an infant together end up going their separate ways. Perhaps we were a statistic too. More on that later.

During Marriage

With my in-laws, there was much more formality and always a hierarchy based on age, gender, and more. I wasn't used to that, and it felt very uncomfortable. I tried my best to adapt.

But here's the thing—especially since I have learned to speak my mind in an unfiltered way.

I don't blame my ex in-laws for being different. I was wrong and naive to assume things would be the same as they were in my family.

Yes, the way I had been conditioned about marriage made me not check on these similarities. After becoming a daughter-in-law, I sort of forced myself to assimilate to the ways of my in-laws. I was trained to do this right from my family home. I honestly realized much later how I didn't feel fully comfortable having this role in my life. I never knew that I had to examine how it would be to live together before agreeing to live together. I met my in-laws the night of the *"kubool hai"* party. Seventeen people at once. They were so kind, warm, friendly, and literally showered me with love, prayers, and gifts. But the first night I met them, we had already said yes. I believed at 26 years of age that I understood enough about people and I thought I could adapt in *any environment* as long as I loved the man I was married to. I realized much later that that was poor judgment on my part. Chalk up my divorce to that, haha. Poor judgment. I'll own that any day over forcing myself to be in a marriage I didn't want to be in. I simply didn't know earlier that it may be wise to dig deeper than that on meeting family ahead of time, etc. And *I had made a choice* to get married. *No one forced me. I made the choice to let it go.*

It has always felt like the right decision. These things are never one-dimensional. Despite the strict rules and control I would come to know, they would show me moments of kindness and genuine love. My first birthday after my wedding, my father-in-law made sure I felt special by saying, "we'll go out to eat today, it's your birthday, pick any restaurant you like." My husband would always make these grand gestures to show he cared, like renting out an entire beach for the occasion. My mother-in-law would make me fresh, hot, homemade lunch every day for work, serve me coconut water when I was unwell, and always encouraged me to spend time with my mom when she came to visit. There was a lot of love and laughter in this life. I embraced it all, and enjoyed so many moments of it, too. I am very grateful to have experienced it. This was not a bitter divorce; with work and patience it felt peaceful between my ex and I. Yes, there were a few challenging conversations with others around us, but my ex and I always had a united front, always had each other's back. For that, I am forever grateful.

Now what could I do when discovering all of this, feeling like I didn't really belong in this new world I had created for myself?

Here's what I decided at year three: Suck it up and live on. Because I loved my husband. It took a traumatic incident of losing our child at year five, and therapy thereafter to stop saying at year seven, "We're different, but it's fine, we can stay married."

I cannot, however, dismiss the small voice saying "what are you doing?" had started to play like a soundtrack in my head even before that traumatic incident. What stopped me from taking action was: my ex was literally the sweetest man. We had great banter, friendship of the purest kind, and shared so much laughter. I didn't want to give up just yet.

I can safely say it was when some family started crossing more and more into our boundaries, and trying to control us from afar more and more, that I just couldn't take it anymore. I didn't leave my semi-controlling home to only be more controlled as an adult and for the rest of my married life too. I told one of the elders during the course of our separation: "If there ever comes a time when he has to pick his family or me, I'm simply going to back away. I don't want to pull him away from his family." This came with the realization that I couldn't blame them or expect them to change who they were. I had to accept that we were simply different, and I didn't have the wisdom at the time of getting married to look into all of that. I didn't like being controlled, and I could see they weren't willing to give me the space to make my own decisions, freely, even being 31 years old. That didn't sit right with me. Now that I knew this fact, I could no longer blame the 'intrusive/controlling' family, because I realized that the responsibility of my happiness lay on me. It was up to me to take responsibility for my life and do something about it. If I wanted it to look and feel different, I had to take action.

That was the other side of the story of controlling family—whom I also loved to bits. I believe my ex's family loved me too, and have their own woes about me. And I'm okay with that. I grieved the loss of my ex's family, as we had made our own individual connections which were separate from the formal relationship of me being married into the family. We developed close personal bonds, kept in touch and cherished one another. We were simply different. So we had to let each other go: on a personal level (ex and I) and overall (family, friends, his and mine, navigating new uncharted unconventional waters). I am so grateful for the love shared at every stage of this journey—be it with my family, my ex's family, friends, loved ones.

This isn't a story about bashing anyone—this story is about me reflecting on how I journeyed into coming into my own, in an imperfect way— playing the leading role in a story that I wrote—one that wasn't written for me by society. And so, it isn't a story attacking my in-laws, my family, community, or society. It's about what I realized on this journey of what I can only describe as a very full life. Full of love, beauty, and some stark realizations, pivots and beautiful lessons.

Contemplating Divorce

At this point, with this awareness, I took the necessary steps to ensure I once again didn't give up on myself and become a martyr. We tried all we could to rectify our situation, including counseling, but I didn't want to be the nagging wife, forcing him to be someone he wasn't, or pressuring myself to be in a family that I felt disconnected from.

We have one life. Our son Hassan's life lasted 65 days, but it felt like 65 years. He fulfilled his purpose on this Earth and departed to the skies. Every day with Hassan was a gift. On the other side of witnessing Hassan's journey was the reality that each day felt extremely precious and significant. I was no longer going to simply *exist to fill a role someone else determined for me*. I was going to live, to *thrive*. Not only that, I was not going to simply *survive* on someone else's terms, I *dared* to wish, to *thrive* on my terms.

I told myself: I'm going to ensure I am surrounded by loving, supportive people, whose support isn't conditional, dependent on me doing everything they want me to do. "We can surely exist with autonomy and unconditional love," I thought to myself. I started to notice how I spoke to and treated myself. No one could treat me badly if I first treated myself well. No one could suppress my opinions unless I did it to myself first. There would be no more fading into the background and suppressing my opinions because "men" or "elders" know better. We can and should all be able to contribute to the decisions that affect our own lives, even if we are young or not men!

It's really an inside-out journey.

The journey starts with blaming others for our unhappiness, being a victim—and then life shows us a mirror that forces us to improve from the inside out. Something I read around that time that contributed to improving how I spoke to myself was a book by Mahfuz Chowdhury called *"Project Reinvention"* that spoke about managing our "internal chatterbox." I keep coming back to ensuring my internal chatterbox has the positive, abundant mindset cassette on loop. Sitting in the pain and processing is of course important, for a reasonable time. But I said to myself: "No more being a victim, No more blaming." I needed to take responsibility for my life and happiness. Another technique I have started applying was one a friend shared recently, a saying: "Ask yourself better questions." Practicing that has also been a game changer. The questions we ask ourselves can say a lot about our mental state and direction.

In making that my new story, I did what I had to do to make sure I expressed myself honestly. This marriage wasn't going to work like this, with so much intrusion, interference, outside control. Our marriage was over. I could no longer be the doormat wife I had been all those years.

While we may not have been suited to be life partners, we surely were friends – the best there ever could be. Why? How?

He saw me, he understood me, and supported me. He literally took me out the first night I wanted to try being hijab-less. We got fried chicken. It was fun. He never once made me feel bad. It's true that the first time I shared with him the previous year that I wanted to remove my hijab, his response was: "We cannot stay married in that case, Mish." But he never judged or shamed me for my decision of removing the hijab, which I really appreciated. A month later, on his own accord, he said to me: "No worries, Mish, you can remove your hijab, and we can stay married." I was elated and grateful.

Around the same time, we were having the conversations around my hijab journey, when I didn't have enough funds to pay my life coach. He literally just gave me the money without me even asking. He paid voluntarily for the very coach who helped me through the process of removing my hijab. That's a great human right there. He was truly supportive, and didn't have a desire to control my curiosity. He got it.

Hijab Journey—Before, During and After Marriage

For 15 years, I wanted to remove my hijab and never did because I assumed that everyone I knew would disown me, and I'd be ostracized. I realized how wrong I was when I finally went up to my dad and told him I wanted to take off my hijab, and he said, "It does not matter what you wear, it matters who you are inside." My mom's reaction was sweet as well, she asked, "Does this mean you're not a Muslim anymore?" with a concerned look—no anger, no judgment, just a genuine question. I was so grateful for that. A few months later, they bought me a bunch of summer dresses. My family accepts me as I am, while they practice faith the way they wish. And it works. I am so grateful. I do not know why I thought it would be so much worse in my head. I know now that I was the one in my own way. I was overthinking it. I never took action on it or even asked. Fear held me back, losing Hassan and having a supportive husband/friend made it so that I had the courage and support to take this step.

So what did that make this—all this so-called mess? It made it my story.

This divorce was about me.

I changed.

My ex honestly didn't. And I do not think it mattered when I decided that I wanted to move on for ME.

He was as nice a husband to me as always. I remember apologizing to him at one point, telling him—I know it's because I changed, and I am sorry I can no longer be the wife I used to be for you for seven years. It is not an easy thing to do. To end a marriage with a perfectly nice man because you know staying with him means abiding by the rules of society that you don't believe in anymore. I didn't want to cause havoc in his life, and he wanted a wife that would participate in the life we had both already been a part of, one that I knew well enough to know I couldn't do it anymore. I no longer wished to be a spectator of my life, to be a doormat and abide by gendered laws in the home, I wanted to be out in the field. I wished for freedom of expression and sharing marital duties in a humane way.

When I got married, I was a different person as compared to who I was when I divorced.

I felt like an 18-year-old at 32 years of age after signing those papers. This was the first time in my life I had the freedom to make my own decisions.

Silenced

When was the first time I was silenced? Or rather, the first time I allowed myself to be silenced.

I was 12. I used to write a daily diary. I thought it was a safe space to record my thoughts. I came home one day to my dad having read it and was dealt a tight slap. I wouldn't write a journal entry again for over 20 years. How could I blame anyone else for silencing me, when I was the very first one silencing myself?

At 14, I moved to Canada and life changed so much. I went from being a child to having real responsibilities. Much of my teens and twenties were spent helping mom raise my younger brother. I was also very involved in the community.

At 16, I experienced sexual abuse at the hands of a friend's father-in-law. A friend who, at the time, was like a sister to me. It was a life-changing experience. I would never be the same. I made myself be "patient" and be the "bigger person" as faith taught me, but I realized I was gaslighting myself. I know now that I was protecting a pedophile.

Sparing your delicate hearts and souls the gory details, I'll say this much: Our families were close, so I was forced to be around him a lot, it went on for a prolonged time, it was horrible, I never told anyone. The lord only knows why I stayed silent. I have no idea. I felt like there was a taala (lock) on my mouth and a heavy suffocation in my heart. I used to speak to my friend Aisha about it, and she was so kind, mature and genuinely there for me.

My parents saw my cell-phone bill skyrocket with international calls between Aisha and I (we were living in Tanzania and Canada then), and asked me what was going on. Mind you, I was probably 17 at this time.

Mom and Dad: Who are you calling so much?

Me: Aisha in Dar

Them: Why?

*Me: *starts sobbing**

Mom and Dad confused

Eventually I find the words to tell them that I was being sexually approached, propositioned, and inappropriately touched by this uncle seen as a father figure.

They consoled me, hugged me, etc. which was nice

But their advice shocked me.

They said something along the lines of: "Don't say anything to anyone, Mish, you are a girl, no one will believe you. Plus, it will ruin your friend's marriage. Your silence will protect her marriage. Don't say anything to anyone."

I did what they asked, but it felt horrible. Maybe the advice was coming from a good place, a protective one, but it really affected me for years after. If I can't kick and scream about sexual abuse, is there much else I *can* kick and scream about? Why do I have to keep it in because I'm a girl? Why did I, a child, essentially, have to protect an adult's feelings? Why did I have to stay silent? I'm being abused, and suddenly it's my job to protect someone's marriage? Make it make sense.

Again, I was silenced to be kept safe. But the choice to stay silent was mine. I felt like I was obeying some abstract rules, fighting the rebellion inside—but I did not know then what I know now about parenting and growing older. I was being protected and shielded from a world that tends to harshly judge and question a trauma survivor. I cannot blame anyone, but I can say this for sure: I understood at a very young age that adults were not always at liberty to do what they thought was right because the world is not black or white—they have to live in those gray shadows and bring up reasonable human beings within that space. I realized at around that time in my life as a child that adults were not perfect, nor were humans, or parents. They were in fact messy, very messy. Parenting in this world can be messy, I realize now. Very messy.

It was like teaching children that they could get hurt when they played outside without adult supervision. No adult wants to tell a child to restrain their natural enthusiasm, but they sometimes choose to. Everything is situational. And the choices that parents make, or what they deem to be unsafe for their child - which in my case was being vocal about the fact that I was being abused – would depend on the individual lens of the parent.

In the similar vein, most parents do not wish their trauma survivor of a child to have to answer questions like, "Did that really happen? How do we believe you? Produce the evidence—let's reopen those scars to examine them."

If you were a parent, would you want your child subject to that?

No.

I didn't understand all this before. I carried a lot of anger for being silenced. And now that I've understood it, the anger is a lot less about being silenced, but there's surely some anger around being abused itself. I don't know if anyone who is violated ever really fully gets over it, honestly.

Let's get back to the story.

Around the time of my divorce, I noticed that my friend's teenage daughter, (the same one whose father-in-law had SA'd me 15 years prior) had gone from being really loud and bubbly to really quiet. I started losing sleep over it for *months*, and arranged for my friend to be notified, not because I wanted justice, but because I wanted her teenage daughter to be safe around this man that I knew had a terrible history. My family stood firmly behind me in support and solidarity. I went ahead. Unfortunately, I was gaslighted by her. Her husband said, "You took it out (verbalized it) after keeping it in for 15 years, now put it back." It was very difficult to digest, as she had been like a sister to me. I found out later that she got her daughter tested for signs of abuse, so clearly the gaslighting was them covering for her father-in-law. How pathetic. I was grateful at the end of the day that the girl was safe, for the support of my family, including my ex, regardless of being gas lit. I slept better knowing her daughter would be safe.

I understood though, through that experience of breaking my silence, that in my silence was my safe space – 15 years belatedly. 16-year-old me may not have been able to bear it all at once, and the gaslighting too. I am now indebted to their advice to stay silent in a sense. Even though I didn't like it- perhaps it was best for that time. I'll never know otherwise. I am not saying sexual abuse does not happen or is not meant to be tackled as a societal evil. But how do I want to show up without expecting my loved ones to put my pain on a pedestal?

That was the root of my anger.

So, my story became my unmet need: to be myself, openly.

I wanted to be with a man who had autonomy over what he does with his life and his time. That's what I knew about my love for freedom when I got married. By the time our marriage ended, I knew something else: I was responsible for creating the space for myself to explore. I had been so focused on breaking the generational curse of wives being an afterthought, that I totally took myself out of the equation when I saw that was never going to change. I couldn't depend on my ex or his family to fulfill my unmet need to be myself openly. That was my own responsibility. I got to work on that once I realized it. Let's backtrack for a second, though:

At age 26 in 2014, I got married to a man within eight months of first meeting him, with only two dates in between, purely because he was a genuinely nice, kind guy, Tanzanian (we spoke all the same languages and really connected culturally) and clearly, to me, then, he had autonomy over his life. My naive self thought that was all I needed to know to marry someone. I thought: "good, finally a guy from "back home" who has a sense of freedom and is actually respectful – and we have banter."

When I moved in with his large family, I was already used to a multi-generational home. We all lived together and honestly, I thought that was a lot of fun. What was different about my ex was, no one asked him where he was going, what time he would be back, what he was doing. So I thought: "Here's a man from a similar culture and family, and he's cool. And he has freedom, so I, in turn, will have freedom if I marry him."

We had a lovely married life together, laughing, connecting, surprising one another, taking a lot of trips and spending days at the beach.

During Separation/Divorce
What triggered our separation?

It was when we visited therapy together after losing our precious baby. Hassan was born in July 2018 and passed away in September 2018 in Toronto. He never left the hospital. My ex and I spent 65 days with him, hoping that he would have a good life. God had other plans, and he is the best of planners. Hassan was a beautiful gift in our lives. Our lives would never be the same after this experience. We both lost ourselves in grief, and therapy helped us find ourselves again. Unfortunately, though, it led to us losing one another—because that is when we realized how different we really are.

Being witness to Hassan's journey together made my ex and I very intensely understand the value of life and each and every single day. We just wanted to do our own thing after all this. And our own things were in vastly different directions, we realized during therapy. I wanted to go to dance classes. He wanted a wife who would do otherwise. I used to be that wife who could show up in ways that made him and his family (and mine) proud, keeping my own interests under wraps. I resorted to dancing in the bedroom and singing under my breath to appease myself. But I didn't want to do that anymore. I wanted to dance like nobody was watching, and sing to my heart's content and as loud as I wanted to. Oh, and, I wanted to feel the wind in my hair. It's a glorious feeling I had craved far too long. Hassan coming into and then leaving this physical life made me fearless, in a way, to what the society would think. I don't see a love for music and dance as a negative thing anymore. Others did.

It's ok to be different. But to hide who I am? I didn't want to anymore. No one was even outright asking me to. I was simply putting myself in that position over and over. It was time to break the cycle.

My ex and I separated in October 2020 without telling our families. We wanted to test it out ourselves before involving everyone else. I started driving Uber while working on finding a job and staying in a room in Toronto near Christie Pits Park. I had sublet it from my friend for a few months, paying $700 for the room I occupied. My ex and I still kept the facade up of being married during this phase, as we figured things out on our own. He and I supported each other. We'd go to family dinners together locally, and even once attended a Zoom birthday party for his uncle, whom I adored. We appeared on video and I didn't have my hijab on.

He supported me. Even though he knew there may be chatter in the family about it.

I really appreciated that moment. We were already apart, he didn't have to, but we were friends, still. And that is something I will always appreciate about our breakup.

By December, two months later, we solidified our decision to go our separate ways, and shared it with our families. They already knew we were having problems, but we saw that it came as a shock to a few that it was actually happening.

When our divorce happened, I felt very silenced by his family. During that time, I told my ex's family member who had interfered a lot in our marriage: "Thank you for the pain, I will turn it into power."

And it has—I'm so much happier for it. This one's for the people who are fed up with the patriarchy and outdated, *ghissa pita* gender roles.

Eid of 2020 was different. My ex and I had spent a year and a half doing all we could to save the marriage, despite being so controlled by a family two oceans away. I was determined that we carve a life of "our own" within the family. When his family was initially controlling at certain moments, directly or indirectly, I would never speak up. The first time I chose to say something was a whopping five years and four months into the marriage. My ex's family member sent me a text saying, "your sister-in-law was there, you shouldn't have gone away for the weekend." This was a significant moment for me. This was them sending me a text because I decided to go away for *one* weekend with my family while being present with my ex-sister-in-law and her child for *literally months*. I didn't even have the freedom to go away for a *weekend?* I didn't have the freedom to *make my own decisions?* I was 31 years old at that time, and it just felt *wrong*.

That's when I realized that they had way too much control over my life.

Flashback to a little over a year into our marriage: my ex and I decided it would be good for our marriage to move out of the extended family home and live alone. When we shared this decision with his parents, they were not happy. As a result of their response, we canceled our plans to move out. In the weeks that came, my ex's elder didn't even look at me, she was so disappointed. My ex wasn't given the same ill-treatment. It was reserved only for me. I remember one time I literally was sitting beside the elder's feet; she was on the couch, I was on the carpet, and we were all chilling in the living room as a family. She didn't even look at me – it was like I didn't exist. I was weeping. She didn't even care. This was a person I had taken as a mother. I had left my loving parents to be treated this way? Moving out was about us, not them, yet they took it personally. Looking back, makes me think, is this how adults really function? Where is the emotional intelligence? Where is the empathy? Why couldn't they view the issue practically instead of taking it personally? The only reason I can think of them not wanting us to move out was to maintain a sense of control over us. I gas lit myself, said to myself it was wrong to even think of moving out. Blamed myself for even daring to suggest it. Back to doormat mode I went, as I had seen women around me doing all their lives.

Then, when the fog cleared, after the separation and before the divorce, I sent a very strongly worded message to my ex's elder explaining that his daughters-in-law aren't just to be controlled, we have our own ideas and opinions too. He never responded. Of course. My thoughts or feelings didn't matter to him. Even in the past when I tried to express myself to him in person, he brushed me off saying "we understand you," without so much as hearing two sentences leave my mouth. They even controlled which language we spoke at home. It was too much. I didn't sign up for all this when I fell in love with my ex. I just wanted to build a life with my husband. Why were they forcing me to change? I couldn't express myself as effectively in Gujarati as in English. I didn't sign up for all this. I married for love. I never expected my speech to be controlled, too. There was no appreciation for the daughters-in-law and how much effort we put in.

Thankfully, my ex and I continued to be on good terms. That gave me a lot of solace. He was the one I initially met, and he and I are the ones who cultivated the relationship, went through grief, and difficult moments together. We were the ones going through the breakup. Everyone else I considered a spectator anyway. Their opinions did not count.

A few months after announcing our divorce to our families, my family started supporting me financially while I worked. They have supported me until very recently, and I am very grateful for that. It allowed me time and space to heal, grow and explore in more ways than I can count. I realize that not everyone has such support during divorce, but I'm happy to report that my family never questioned or ostracized me for my decision. It was beautiful, honestly, how accepting they were. I told them about my divorce and, an hour later, we were laughing and playing Monopoly Deal. Life goes on. They never made me feel bad about it. My extended family/friends and his were all positive and supportive. All in all, I'd say we had quite a smooth divorce compared to many stories I have encountered, and I'm grateful we had a good bond when we walked away.

Flash forward to now:

After Divorce

I felt supported by so many of my friends, and family. They accepted me even without my hijab. I now dance when, where, and how I want. I wear what I want, I sing, speak my mind freely, and I am so, so grateful for it. I have been imperfect and made mistakes with decisions in my new-found independent life, but still, the hardest day post-divorce is still easier than any day married or prior to being married. Because I can make my own choices. I had to go through this journey to arrive at where I am, and I am so grateful. I am also starting a steady job in exactly seven days; I'm ecstatic and grateful for this next chapter of my journey!

Therapy changed my life. I read this somewhere recently:

> *"If you don't address your childhood trauma, your adult relationships will. When you look for a partner to heal your emotional wounds, you will keep manifesting the same relationships."*
>
> *-Author Unknown*

This happened in my life in such a real way. I thought I left my problems behind when I left my marriage behind. I thought they were the problem. Boy, was I naive. I was definitely the problem.

Being divorced gave the illusion that the control over my life was all done. But the truth is: it wasn't. I was still putting myself in the same situation except this time it wasn't with in-laws, it was with friends, or relationships. That's why I say it was no one's fault—but it is *my responsibility now* to notice patterns and work to improve/fix them.

Yes, the Desi community has flaws, and we are indoctrinated with *"log kya kahenge"* (what will people say).

But I ran from that a long time ago, in 2018 when Hassan passed, and I couldn't give a rat's ass *ke log kya kahenge* to be honest.

Plus, I've noticed that this doesn't just happen in the Desi community. It happens in many families/communities around the world.

The question is—where do we go from here? Once we clearly see what we cannot unsee?

Where I go from here, is to live this life to the fullest, make my own decisions (responsibly), and live a fantastic life, and that is that.

What's your plan?

There are two Misriyas in my story.

The Misriya of the then. And the Misriya in the now.

The Misriya of the then did wonder about boundaries, sometimes aloud, and she did try to see how it would feel to test them. She may not have followed through with actual action, but the questions and the wonderment were there. The feeling that there was something beyond those boundaries, and not just damnation of some sort, was always there. Was it exciting? Was it a kind world? Was it a world I would fit into? There was more of that than fear of venturing out. I craved being outside my world because in my world it felt like I had no real autonomy or freedom. No rights.

Yet, the Misriya of then did not know that she had choices.

And so, she convinced herself that if she just stayed within the boundaries – if she just colored within the lines, if she shied away from colors that were too bright or would bring too much attention her way – she would be happy.

Because everyone around her would be happy.

She was busy co-creating life from what she knew—which was limited.

Whether it was parents or grandparents or in-laws…they all influenced her voice with the best intentions.

The Misriya who lives in the here and now is a very different person.

She has found happiness outside those boundaries and created a beautiful work of art with colors that she hand-picked—and outside the lines that were drawn for her. Those were battle lines to her. Now, there is just free flowing love.

This Misriya comes armed with lessons she learned from being the Misriya of the Then.

And this is the story of how the child within taught the adult.

Here are a few things I realized:

Internalizing the pain and guilt over the years led to bottled-up anger and emotions, and the inability to emotionally regulate. I could keep myself strong in taking up major responsibilities, but as soon as I was triggered, related to sexual abuse, I turned into a pile of mess. I regressed to being a child who literally needed to be cared for. Who threw a tantrum. My poor family and close friends have had to deal with my random spouts of anger that came up in relation to that. Then about a week later, when I have moved through my trigger, I'd do an apology tour. It had been exhausting, and it stopped me from cultivating deeper relationships with new people I met. I kept people at arm's length because of my pain.

However, it's also true that my closest loved ones who have stuck with me through this have taught me so much, and we have shared so much happiness too, not just dark times. I'm honestly humbled by it all and thankful for each of the souls that have touched my life. I thought I had it all figured out, but since my divorce and since the freedom to think for myself and actually express myself, I have had some extremely messy moments. I have also had some incredibly beautiful, remarkable moments. And I'm grateful for it all. And better for it. Life has humbled me. And the process of writing this chapter and getting triggered multiple times over the last six months has too. I can say it was all worth it, because I'm a better person now. I learned a lot from this entire journey, starting from 16.

And now I'm giving myself permission to continue right from age 16. Where I left the unscathed version of *moi*. I'm giving myself the grace, space, and freedom to simply explore life as if I was 16. Yay!

Your turn next—what's your story?

Why are you reading this book?

Sending you love and well wishes, *Asante Sana* for reading.

Thank you, truly, for everything to each soul reading this that has touched my life, and whose life I have had the pleasure of visiting/ witnessing. I pray our effect on each other is net positive in the long run.

Love,

Mish <3

Misriya is a soul having a human experience. She lives and works in Toronto. She is a multi-passionate person, with a background in dental hygiene and custom bridal clothing. She currently works in banking while making spice blends and Oudh in her spare time for Tah's Tasty and Oudh Dreams. Comedy is a passion of hers, she has been performing since June 2024. She is a huge fan of dancing and music, and regularly attends classes. This is her second published work, the first one being a chapter titled "Breathe," in the book *See You Again* where she wrote about how she dealt with the grief related to losing her son, and how that shaped her to be the person she is today.

Born to Rise: A Story of Escape and Empowerment

PREET JOHAL

He didn't even spare the most important moment of my life; when my daughter was born.

I was overdue, and we had to leave for the hospital early in the morning to be induced. The day started so perfectly, I packed all the little things to bring the baby home. It felt like the happiest day of my life. My husband took pictures of my belly. I was so happy and excited in my loose red and blue maternity dress that I picked to bring home my baby girl.

As we were driving to the hospital, he started asking me for updates about our trucking dispatch business and how much billing I still have pending. Although I was working until the night before, he was already unhappy about my upcoming downtime after giving birth.

We reached the hospital, and as we were in the waiting area, he jokingly said, "You'll give birth today and tomorrow you should be ready to get back to the office," with a smirk. I vividly remember his devilish look and the knot that formed in my gut at that moment, but I could only smile back at him.

It was a mix of fear and avoidance of reality to keep the peace. I just wanted to meet my baby and pretend as if his craziness didn't exist.

That was the only way to experience some moments of joy and happiness.

Once I was admitted, I was given medication to be induced, and I was in labor the whole night with intense pain and contractions. During this time, no one was there with me. My mom and dad had disowned me for marrying out of caste, waiting for me to fail and collapse. My sister-in-law decided to move out exactly a week before my delivery date. My husband was there, with stacks and stacks of paperwork for the trucking company, and all night, I kept hearing paper shuffling. It felt like he was making more noise, as the contractions were getting more intense.

Somehow, I survived the night and early in the morning, I gave birth to an angel. My husband was nowhere to be seen during my delivery. Apparently, he had left the room because he said he couldn't watch the pain and blood.

Surprisingly enough, as soon as I held my daughter and saw her beautiful and peaceful face, I forgot everything I had been through.

Just looking at her face, I felt an indescribable connection and wholeness. I just wanted to savor the moments of being a new mom and fully live those moments. But then reality hit as my husband came back into the room and looked at me with the same devilish smile. He started telling me how much work he got done last night. He was the master of stealing the joy out of every good moment.

I knew my daughter's life would not be like mine.

But I had also tried to prevent my life from turning out like my mom's.

A little girl, with simple dreams and in pursuit of joy—every time I saw an airplane fly above me, it felt as if my dad was there. I used to think America was somewhere up there—high in the sky, and that's why airplanes take people to America, where my dad was. Meeting my dad someday was a big dream. I believed he would show up in the village and punish all the bad people who hurt me and my mom. I imagined him taking us to some kind of heaven called America. I was the youngest of my cousins in the village and always felt scared and intimidated.

I remember one of my male cousins slapped me when I was about seven or eight years old, riding on my bicycle from school. I started crying and kept riding. My cheek felt so much heat coming out of it because his slap was so hard. I don't remember what I did to deserve that slap, all I remember is being quiet and crying. He was much older than me, maybe by seven or eight years, and his height alone was intimidating. He was stronger than me, too. I told my mom about it, and I have no memory of him facing any consequences for it. My mom always told me to stay quiet and to not go places where I could get in trouble because my dad wasn't there, no one would protect me if anything happened.

Of course, I listened to my mom. She was all I had. I obeyed her when she told me to stay quiet. I always wanted to make her happy. Many times, people had touched me inappropriately and in my gut I knew something was wrong, but I was supposed to stay quiet. My mom had conditioned me to believe that if I ever spoke up then I would create problems for her, and because I loved my mom, I did what I was told to do. But my little brain knew something was wrong, and I believed that my dad would rescue us someday.

Looking up at the passing airplanes was so satisfying because I could believe that everything was going to be better someday.

But when that plane bearing my father landed, it was a jarring shock, a rude awakening, rather than the pleasant reunion that I had always craved. Far from keeping me safe, I found out that he was the last person that I could depend on.

The morning after he arrived, my first sight of him was of his form, bent over and vomiting from excessive alcohol consumption.

That was my first memory of the man who I thought would rescue us. That was my first impression of what I did not want my man to ever be.

Even though I was so young, these were the moments that shaped me. These were the moments that showed me that I needed to escape. And that is where many of my choices eventually came from.

From a very young age, I viewed my mom as a victim who sacrificed her life serving my dad and his family's needs, taking his abuse on a daily basis and yet maintaining an image of a perfect family. Even worse, covering up his deceitful acts so he had good standing in society.

I had always tried to save her and protect her from my dad. My dad was a monster inside the house, while outside, he pretended to be very soft-spoken and respectful to others. He still disrespected my mom around family and friends, and it was considered normal. There were few times I remember my aunties consoling my mom because my dad put her down and insulted her in front of them. Despite the support she got from other women, my only take on the matter as a 16-year-old was that she should leave him instead of enduring all the pain and suffering.

But she did not leave him. She could not even fathom that. Her life was consumed by that phrase, "What would people say?"

I did not want that trap.

I didn't want to be like my dad or to associate with anyone like him. I certainly did not want to marry anyone like him—an irresponsible alcoholic. I hated him so much, his arrogance, his stupidity, his fakeness, and his anger. He was such a shallow person, completely empty inside himself. To feel his manhood, he needed to belittle my mom in every way possible.

As I got older, he would use every little mistake I made against my mom to further bring her down by saying, "Our daughter is like that because of your incompetence."

He lacked responsibility, respect, honesty, and integrity in every way. Yet, he expected everyone in the house to treat him with utmost respect and obey his law and order.

These circumstances were suffocating and made me want to run away from home. My home life also made me determined to work hard for my dignity and respect. I was intent on creating a better life for myself, a happier, and financially abundant family.

When I was nineteen, I learned from a friend about online chat rooms and how you could talk to people anonymously. It was a good feeling to connect with others and be vulnerable without being exposed.

During one of those adventures online, I connected with a guy who seemed really funny, silly and made me laugh. Bubbling with laughter was a new thing to me. We never laughed at home. It wasn't allowed. Laughter was seen as some kind of threat to my dad losing control over my mom and mom losing control over me.

Now, with my newfound refuge, I felt more and more alive. Each time he made me laugh, and I wanted more of those happy feelings. Before cell phones were common, I had no way of calling him without getting caught by my parents. He gave me an 800 number to call from pay phones. I felt so special. For the first time, someone did something for me and created a convenience for me. I liked the feeling of being taken care of. I felt like he sees me, cares for me, wants to talk to me and listen to me. I started calling him regularly and every time, he was waiting for my call. I started looking forward to our conversations.

These soft feelings made me feel more like a girl. Being taken care of by someone was a beautiful feeling that I didn't want to release. Life was getting better and prettier day by day, and I wanted more of it. In a few months of phone conversations, I was learning so much about him. He was driven. Hardworking. He was the exact opposite of my dad. I took that as a sign that it was all going in the right direction. When I met him for the first time, he told me he didn't drink alcohol. It felt like I hit the jackpot.

This was a total dream-come-true scenario. I was sure I had finally met my soulmate. The one who would rescue me. We decided that we were made for each other, and we made a promise to get married.

He was the exact opposite of my dad in many ways. But only in the ways I was looking for. I thought what I needed was financial stability. But I later realized in marriage, there is so much more. I had not seen anything beyond my parents' marriage to know how much more could go wrong with me.

My parents were my only benchmark, unfortunately.

And those same parents refused to accept the choice I had made. Their excuse? He was from a lower caste. When I disclosed to my parents that I wanted to marry this guy from California, my father furiously got up from the couch and said, *"Tere tou eh umeed nai si!"* [I did not expect this from you]. This was only because the guy I mentioned was not a Jatt.

My dad's exact words were, *"Jatt hona chaheda chahe mangta hee hove."* He must be of the same caste, even if he's homeless.

Since my dad flat-out rejected this alliance, a year later I decided to leave home and get married to the person I believed was the love of my life. It felt like freedom from a suffocating environment that was filled with chaos. I had no idea I was just moving from one hell into another.

That was 2003.

When I look back, I can't believe I lived in that hell for 16 years, hoping it would get better someday. That someday never came. Instead, every aspect of my life was getting worse with time. How naive I was. I was losing my sense of self with the constant confusion, betrayal, control, and subjugation. He literally changed the day we got married. He was no longer the person who expressed love and care towards me. Suddenly, he became demanding, controlling, wanting everything his way. Everything needed to happen at his timing. It didn't feel so bad at first because he was hardworking, and I was conditioned to appreciate and recognize his efforts.

His anger started very early on; he would completely break me down with insults and taunts. When I would be totally shattered, he would come back, apologize, and, sometimes, promise not to do that again.

That's how good girls were supposed to be—do anything and everything to meet your husband's needs, make him comfortable, and allow him to lash out at you, because men do that sometimes. I was overworking and over-functioning just to prove myself to others. At the same time, I allowed myself to believe that I did not have any rights. Hence, it was my job to remain calm and positive and ignore the disrespect, the demeaning side comments, the making fun of me in front of others and calling it all a joke.

2014 was the year the Universe woke me up.

We were living in a castle of sorts. A house on top of a hill with no neighbors nearby. No neighbors to even hear me scream. I was not entirely sure if we had made it in life, or if I was being strategically isolated from everything that could pull me back to safety. To the point where, in sheer arrogance, he fired gunshots into the air. If I died there, no one would know. I knew things had to change, but I never wanted to file for divorce.

One morning at 7 a.m., as I approached the bathroom sink to brush my teeth, I noticed a big smile on my husband's face while he was looking at his phone. Considering his grumpy nature, a big smile came across like a huge red flag. As I leaned over to see his phone, he said, look who texted me. It was his ex-wife from 11 years ago. He only said that because he knew I had seen the name flash across the phone.

The tone in his voice indicated he was concerned about her, and stupid me went along with his story and asked him if she was okay. In my intuition, I felt something was off, but I wasn't courageous enough to listen to that voice of guidance and truth inside of me. Within a month, I found myself in another chaos on top of all the craziness I was already dealing with.

He was hellbent on confusing me and manipulating me into thinking that I had no basis for doubting him. But more than that, I was scared of violence coming back as a reply to any questioning that I might indulge in. I was simply programmed to take his word and trust him blindly. For my own safety, more than anything else.

His soul-crushing abuse began when I got pregnant, just a few months after marriage. Sometimes, I find myself speechless, with no words to describe my feelings and my experience. As I am writing this, I can still hear my gut screaming at me from 20+ years ago.

RUN RUN RUN…………..

But I didn't know where to go. I had just escaped from another hell in the hopes of building a peaceful home. I was giving everything I had to build my new home with pure love, care, affection, and hard work.

At times, he was very affectionate, and then suddenly he would turn into a monster. My little brain and tender heart couldn't make sense of it. I wanted to believe it was love because I was starved for love. I don't know how I became so strong, so brave, and immensely tolerant to everyday abuse. My head is hurting now as I am writing this. I know I am angry deep down for the injustice.

If not for the lack of care and support from my parents, especially my mom, I would not have endured that so-called marriage. Had I received the love I deserved as a little girl, I wouldn't have been so deprived and needy to run off with this guy and stay with him tolerating all I did.

The shame was over encompassing. Whether it was my parents or me.

Now I graduated from shame to fear. At this point, fear had become the tone of my marriage. Even when he was in a good mood—especially when he was in a good mood—I would become even more fearful. Whether he was berating me, or romancing me, or even firing gunshots in the air to intimidate me—the monotony of my marriage was hinging on my last shreds of sanity and a nervous system that was not entirely regulated. Panic was a staple in my life. Anything he did made me run and hide behind a panic or anxiety attack, oftentimes believing that I fully deserved all of it.

In reality, he had emotionally weakened me with his abuse. Here are a few precious gems of what he would throw my way:

"Shukar kar tere te ticket nai laaye mein."
"He could have turned me into a prostitute, and I should be happy he didn't."

He would say this over and over and over.

"Tere vargiya nu koi pushda nai, shukar kariya kar mein rakheya a tenu."
"No one wants a woman's life. Be thankful I made you my wife."

"I will get you naked and throw you out the window."

"Office makeup kehde laye kar k janni aa…saun wele red lipstick laya kar jado mein hunda va ethe."
"Who do you do makeup for in the office? Wear red lipstick at night when I am here."

I felt immense shame and sadness when he said these things. And worse of all, I felt I deserved it. I wanted to talk to someone, but I had no one to turn to. Even if I did, I don't know if I could bring myself to actually share what was happening.

Why didn't I just leave him?

I couldn't leave because I was afraid of society's judgements. I was afraid of losing the image of a PERFECT family. I was afraid of the shame and embarrassment. I was afraid of not being believed. I was afraid of being alone, I was afraid that the kids would lose their family, I was afraid of being exposed that the portrayal of my life was a lie. And I was afraid that he would make my life even harder and punish me further for exposing him, which he did. I now have a permanent restraining order and a criminal protective order against him. He still continuously violates the restraining orders and finds ways to harass me. I didn't believe I was capable of keeping myself and my children comfortable.

I had actually tried to leave him many times since 2014. On numerous occasions, I would pack stuff for kids and myself and stay in a hotel room. The whole process was traumatizing. Each time, I would leave, dragging the kids with me ensuring that I have everything they need in my car, for their school and studies. I still can't believe I did this for years. He would call, and beg me for hours and hours, touching my feet and apologizing, making new promises, calling himself a *shit person.*

Every time, his apology was more convincing, and I was getting weaker and more exhausted. Of course, I would come back with some new hope. Life would be stable for a month, a week, sometimes just a few days until another episode happened. He knew very well that I wouldn't leave right away again, because he had depleted me. The entire soul-crushing cycle began again. Every time, it was supposed to be a new start, and I told myself I must forgive him, and I must give my 1000% again. Why? Because he apologized.

Yet, only I knew my suffering, abuse, disrespect, and the insults. I remember looking out the window one day, feeling so helpless, and thinking of my mom's curse that I'd never be happy.

"Tere vargiya kadi nai vas sakdiya."
"Girls like you never manage to make a home."
One day, standing by the window, these words felt so real and sharp, as if I deserved the life I was living. It was one of those days, when I was loathed with shame and embarrassment for my decisions, that I just wished the ground beneath me would open and take me in.

I was just too tired and exhausted to even breathe.

Then my son, my ray of light, filled with innocence and curiosity, walked into the room, and held my hand to take me downstairs. Looking at the joy on his face gave me strength again, but from that day onward, I started thinking and observing my life a bit closely. I knew I wasn't going to live in this chaos forever.

I finally had to make a choice.

He had taken things a step too far.

In fact, he began forcing me to do drugs with him. Of all the things that could rob me of; my sanity. He may have been taking drugs before—I may not have known.

Spiritually and morally, it was a very tough thing to fathom. I was already emotionally weak, and taking drugs makes you lose even more control on your fortitude and thoughts. It weakened me even more. I felt like he was gradually making me weaker. The drugs were taking over my body and my mind was diminishing. In this short, temporary fog—my life changed. Because here, my inner voice told me, he would actually kill me. I was convinced of it.

This is the time when I reached out, and I spoke with someone at work and finally, with the support I had, I was finally able to do what needed to be done.

I filed for divorce in August 2019. I felt a sense of joy signing the divorce petition, as if my heart knew that I was starting a journey to REAL freedom. Immediately after filing, I moved out of the castle-like home into a two-bedroom apartment with my kids. I was so terrified of his anger, that I felt if I stayed in the house which he had the keys for, someday he would come and kill me. I was traumatized by his anger to that degree.

Soon after this move, my healing was to begin. It transformed me completely, showing me the full extent of what I had endured, often swinging wildly between grief and rage. At other times, there was raw fear. So many questions.

Why me? And how had I not seen it before? Why had I waited so long?

I remember standing on the balcony of my apartment with tears running down my face and neck, asking God: what have I done to deserve this life? I had just moved out of a mansion that had seemed so real a minute ago. Was I going to return to what I had escaped from?

I felt so broken and had no idea how to move forward. While I was not his victim any longer, I was still unclear what to replace it with.

I prayed to the universe to show me the way. With my complete surrender to the source, I started seeing the light, and little by little, miracles happened. The people I needed on my healing journey were beside me. God gave me the ability to see the good from the bad and the right from the wrong.

Very quickly, I started to realize my blessings—the good people in my life who supported me, encouraged me, and uplifted me.

It took just one man's genuine support to restore my faith in life and humanity. He was not Punjabi, not Sikh, not even Indian, and looked nothing like the men I was conditioned to trust. He was loud, clear, direct, and courageous, with a heart of gold. He helped me see my own worth in ways I never had before.

After a world of hassle through the judicial system, I was able to get a permanent restraining order against my ex, but even that wasn't enough. He violated the restraining order on numerous occasions by stalking and harassing me. I then had to apply for a criminal protective order, which was granted. But that didn't stop him either. He continued to harass me by following my car, sending me notes through people, leaving notes on my car, and having his relatives and people from the Punjabi community call me and my parents to exert emotional pressure.

To my surprise, despite knowing his evil and deceitful acts, every single person from the community who called me said the exact same things, "Keep your family together.", "Go back for the kids.", "Men do these things." etc. His aunt actually said that I should know men are not monogamous.

Within a few months, I realized how quickly my own community alienated me. Not a single person had any compassion for me. They all treated me like I was made out of steel with no emotions. 95% of the people who reached out to me with terrible advice to, "Go back to hell," were men.

And they would be offended when I turned down their shitty advice.

What happened to all the women I knew?

Even these so-called "modern" women are expected to be small, submissive, scared, and take orders from men in their family.

It took an immense amount of courage, over and over, to keep going, and we all have that strength and courage.

Finally, I am now able to celebrate the miracle that happened when I decided to leave all that abuse and toxicity behind.

I was able to create a life where I did not need escape. One that did not reduce my status in my own existence or in my own home. I had broken a generational curse.

Today, my transformation is so complete that I am able to coach women in similar situations to find themselves and a way out to a happy, joyful life that is filled with peace and prosperity.

In helping women see what I made of myself, I am able to help them envision a better life for themselves. By turning into an Empowerment and Transformation Coach, I am able to not only further my own life's purpose—but I can experience the reward of letting go of all the toxicity and abuse, every time I help someone overcome the same.

In my mind, this is my true happy ending.

Preet Johal is a relationship and self-discovery coach, the owner and founder of Ambreesh Cosmetics, and a successful real estate investor. Her journey has been one of resilience and transformation—overcoming intense abuse and thriving after escaping a narcissistic marriage. Driven by a passion for helping others, she rebuilt her life from the ground up, not just surviving but thriving. In her coaching practice, Preet empowers women to break free from toxic relationships, establish healthy boundaries, and reconnect with their authentic selves. Her approach is deeply personal, rooted in the lessons she learned through her own struggles, and she offers practical tools to help women rise above fear, obligation, and guilt. She believes that every woman deserves a life of confidence, self-worth, and empowerment.

In addition to her coaching, Preet expresses her creativity and commitment to empowerment through Ambreesh Cosmetics, a brand she created to inspire confidence and celebrate individuality.

As a real estate investor, she also exemplifies financial independence and success, encouraging her clients to pursue their own dreams with resilience and clarity. Her mission is to show women that life beyond survival is possible—one filled with purpose, freedom, and the power to truly flourish.

From Pain to Spain

MANNY KAUR

Two things I thought I'd never do: get a tattoo and get a divorce. Why? Because good Indian girls don't do that. Now I'm stuck with a tattoo of that dog.

The dog who helped me escape from hell.

If I were to tell my story in a nutshell, here's how it would read:

My dog pooped on my mother-in-law's prayer mat—a dog she never wanted in the first place. Guess who got kicked out?

Spoiler: It wasn't the dog!

It was me.

Who am I?

I was the stereotypical good girl—good grades, good university, didn't talk to boys, dressed modestly, responsible, obedient and a role model for my siblings and cousins. It was always 'Look at Manny.' With all those praises, I thought I was doing life right. I naturally fell into the role of a people pleaser to ensure I didn't anger my father or bring disrespect to the family name. By keeping quiet and keeping my head down, I was able to avoid ruffling any feathers.

It took me a long time and going away to university to eventually shed a few layers of the shy-girl persona. I made new friends and I felt like I fit in. I wasn't just the shy nerdy girl anymore. I liked this newfound confidence and era of self discovery. Then this charismatic, fun guy appeared, making my life all the more exciting.

Soon, my life would go from happily ever after to happily never after.

One spontaneous day, I went with a friend to a gathering. Little did I know I had just walked into my future husband's home. Nothing transpired that night. No sparks were felt. No curiosity from my end. The thought of him didn't even cross my mind. But then I get a "poke" (an antiquated Facebook function to nudge a person without a message or friend request).

I didn't take any action. But then one day, feeling the pressure of marriage from my family, my friends, and societal expectations, add to that a lack of dating experience, I decided to poke back. I felt like I was falling behind and I wasn't even 25. This led to a flurry of messages and eventually to our first date. We went on a romantic date to this cute rustic home that was converted into an Italian restaurant. We were vibing and shared many similar experiences and values growing up. He was hitting the mental checklist I had created based on my parent's and cultural expectations.

From that moment on, we chatted and texted incessantly and spent every moment possible together when he wasn't traveling for work. His charisma was captivating. He was fun and exciting, the life of the party. It was an exhilarating time and I had so many new experiences with him. He made these grand romantic gestures and I felt so special. I thought: *this is the way love is meant to feel like.*

A couple weeks into dating, he told me he loved me. A month into dating, his mom had a serious cancer scare. At our dinner date, he presumptively said, "before she dies, we will have to get married."

The intensity of the relationship had swept me off my feet and I was head over heels for this guy. I didn't even have time to pause and reflect on the relationship. I didn't have the knowledge to pick up on these initial red flags—the misogynistic jokes that I was accustomed to hearing in Desiculture, the love bombing with extravagant gifts and sweet talk. Here I was, years later, married to him, wondering, how did it get to this?

You aren't someone I recognize anymore. You look like you're broken and running on autopilot. I understand you feel stuck and dead inside and you're trying your best to keep your head above water. You move like a zombie. I can see the pain in your face that you try to conceal with a smile. I know you're burdened with a million thoughts - What can you do to make things better? What can you do to make them love you? How can you change? What if you just cook for the family, take care of the house, keep your mouth shut, put your head down, and do what they say, then maybe there will be no more fights, then maybe they will be happy with you.

But what you can't see is that things are never going to change. They are going to get worse! Yes, there are going to be obstacles to get to the exit, but there is an exit and life is going to be much more beautiful on the other side of that door! Why are you the only one trying to change, improve, compromise, and adapt? It's supposed to be a team effort. It's not only your burden to bear.

Wake up! I want to shake you and tell you that this isn't the way it has to be. This isn't the way it should be. You can't win this fight, and what are you even fighting for? You deserve to be loved, you deserve compassion, you deserve partnership. Even he could see it when he'd tell you, "you're too good for me." There is no need to erase yourself and allow them to make you their masterpiece that they're never quite satisfied with. Instead, find that exit and let yourself shine bright. Let the wind blow through your hair and let it take you on many adventures.

Go on ... leave!

If only it was that simple. The D word meant some heavy considerations. First, who thinks about divorce when you're imagining a whole life together? Second, there were good times, the whole relationship wasn't bad. Third, my naivety and timidity was the perfect concoction for manipulation.

He complimented me, acknowledged me, treated me well, made me feel special, important, and wanted! I felt on top of the world. I had finally gotten it right and now I would just have to keep up the role of the perfect wife and daughter-in-law. The highest of praises gave me that push to continue. And then BOOM, I'd slip up, or make some minor mistake that would set him off. I'd fight back, try to justify, try to apologize, but none of that mattered. I was silenced until I accepted the blame.

Any time he lost something—which was often—all hell would break loose. He would cause a ruckus by yelling and appeared very perplexed running all over the house, disturbing everyone's peace and quiet, making it seem like you must drop everything and help him search. He would ask me where his passport was, where his jewelry was, his ID, his car keys, his wallet, etc., and if I didn't know where it was, he would get angry with me because apparently being responsible for those items was a woman's job—his mom had been doing it for years. So I would frantically go searching for it, thinking maybe I did put it somewhere and forgot. I would drop everything including my work and look. I would tear the house apart. Oftentimes it was just an item he misplaced in the most obvious but obscure corner of the house. Then he would just laugh it off—meanwhile he had yelled at me and sent me into a complete frenzy.

Most of these mistakes were so trivial, so I was never sure what would set him off. I was walking on eggshells. This rollercoaster of emotions played its toll on me, and each time there was a drop, my light was dimmed some more until I was just a shell of my existence.

But it didn't feel like reason enough to leave. It had to be something major, like him hitting me.

I remember very early on expressing that hitting me would be a dealbreaker. I had witnessed physical abuse growing up and I knew I would not stand for it. I remember the look of helplessness—a look I would later see in my own eyes. My ex reassured me he would never lay a hand on me and how he was against domestic violence against women.

I also bore witness to emotional abuse growing up, but in comparison, the emotional abuse didn't seem so bad. I felt like I could take this. This behavior was so normalized in our culture—this is how men express their frustration and anger, but they still loved their families. After all, I saw it happen in my own family and despite the abuse these women were the glue of the family. Looking back, they must have been using Super Glue.

I didn't know when it happened, but the emotional abuse got to such an extreme that I had grown numb to it. I remember at the beginning, I would fight back, I'd try to explain myself, but I was shut down every time or given the silent treatment. I cried in front of him a million times, which only agitated him more—"Man up," he would say. "Oh my God, here we go again," or "stop playing victim," were the phrases he would use over and over again. He saw my vulnerability as an annoyance and he needed me to stop.

I remember when I wouldn't really understand what I did wrong and I would have to play the guessing game—apologizing for something I wasn't even sure about. Eventually he said, "your sorrys mean nothing, it's about your actions." Half the time I couldn't even comprehend what I was sorry about, but I wanted him to stop yelling, I wanted him to stop talking down to me. My voice would start to tremble, or my hands would shake as I tried to text back to his latest tirade.

The ex: "Did you not get Dad a Father's Day card, please say you did?"

Manny: "No, I didn't, I thought we were giving him a jersey."

The ex: "Who doesn't give a card on Mother's or Father's Day regardless of a gift?"

Manny: "But I did get Mom one, a very beautiful one."

The ex: "So u get Mom one, what about dad?"

Manny: "You said it was stupid and I shouldn't have."

The ex: "I'm fucking choked. No I didn't, that's a lie about the card. You never mentioned or talked about it with me."

Manny: "No when I got Mom one you said it was stupid."

The ex: Usually when someone lends you money and it's Father's Day , you say thank you with a card."

Manny: "Ok."

The ex: "Ok. Mental illness. It's like when girls get married, they make an effort with their new family."

Manny: "Every birthday, every event I ask you what we should do and you never have anything to say but get mad and say figure it out."

The ex: "Sorry. I thought like every other wife in the world gets it but you."

I changed up my strategy towards the end of the marriage, I would just remain quiet and let him take it all out on me. This didn't sit well with him either—"Are you just going to stand there with that dumb look on your face?" I was so confused! I asked him to tell me what he wanted me to do or say to make things better. You didn't want me to explain myself, as I was just making up excuses in your eyes. *You didn't want me to apologize because they were empty apologies to you. You didn't want me to cry because I was playing victim and it was a weakness in your eyes. And you didn't want me to be quiet, because you didn't like not getting a reaction or a rise out of me. So tell me what you want from me?*

I slowly realized it didn't matter what approach I took. It was easier to be silent. This was the easiest for my psyche and to cut the screaming in my face short. With him, I always just felt like I was in trouble, like some little child. My silence bothered him because he was frustrated by the lack of my reaction, he'd clench his fists and scream with agitation, "Aaahhhh, I wish I could just hit you."

He didn't hit me, so I stayed and endured his taunts, insults, and nagging. To me, this just felt like how it was supposed to be. I was a confident, strong, independent woman and I thought I could handle it. I genuinely felt like I didn't have it so bad in comparison to others, so I diminished my experience. To think that emotional abuse is so normalized in our community, that it wasn't reason enough to justify leaving.

Don't get me wrong, the words definitely hurt. After all, he had called me stupid enough times that I started to believe it. I knew I wasn't. Facts were in front of me. I had an education. I worked at a top firm. I was good with my finances. People were practicing affirmations and I was repeating "I am not stupid, I am not stupid…" Over time, he stripped me of my confidence until I felt so small and unworthy. The confident girl era was a distant memory by this point.

One day, my friend texted me, "I have something to tell you, but I'm not sure if I should say something." At that moment, my heart sank. That sentence revealed nothing, yet I knew what she was going to tell me. It was something I had my suspicions about, but always pushed out of my mind. She told me she had found my husband on Bumble and Tinder.

I went up to him confidently and asked him about the profile. With proof in hand, he couldn't deny it or make me feel crazy. He just rolled his eyes and said, "Oh my God." He weaved this crazy story and I pushed back, but it was pointless; he stuck to his story. I dropped it because he wasn't going to fess up and I was leaving the next day to visit my family.

On my visit, alarm bells were going off. All I could think of was that his story didn't line up, but again, being the good girl, I kept it to myself. I arrived at the airport dreading my return. I was deep in my thoughts when the airline announced that there was a delay. With time to waste, I decided to try and log on to his Facebook. I was not prepared for what I was about to see. I saw message after message to different girls and messages to his friends bragging about his sexual escapades.

Alas, I was on the plane with only time to think. Nowhere to escape. All I could do was huddle up and cry. He wasn't going to be back for another couple weeks from work. I obsessively looked at incoming and outgoing messages, I couldn't tear myself apart, even though it was tearing me up inside. It was gut-wrenching to find out that I didn't even know the extent of his cheating. It started before we were even married.

All of this made me question if he ever even loved me. I expressed that I was thinking of leaving and he begged me not to leave as he didn't want to be exposed. He proposed that he would kill himself so that way I could be a "*bichari* and not a *kanjari*."

Instead of doing the logical thing, accepting reality as truth and seeing him as someone who had acted unfaithfully, I looked inwards at my potential flaws to help understand why he would have cheated. If I could just pinpoint the issue and fix it, then this marriage could be saved.

Being cheated on really messed with my head. It came with so many confusing thoughts and feelings:

Am I not attractive enough?
Do I not turn him on?
Am I not good in bed?
Am I unable to meet his needs?
I was disgusted and repulsed by him. How could he betray my trust? What about all those times I suspected something was off. (Such as not answering his phone/texts until much later, or getting defensive when I casually asked about his plans, his answer was always, "don't worry about it.")

Yet he denied it, "what are you talking about?" he would say. How could he put me at risk of STIs sleeping with all these women, some of whom were sex workers (escorts, prostitutes)? I also felt ashamed that I was cheated on.

What will people think of me?
Maybe she's not putting out?
She couldn't keep her man satisfied!
There must be a flaw in her that makes her cheatable.

At the same time, I felt like I needed to prove him wrong. I wanted to feel desired and I was desperate to please him. I needed to step up my game. That meant dressing up and using makeup more often, it meant figuring out what he felt was missing in the bedroom that he needed to look for elsewhere. I also thought I should try harder to lose weight. It was often a remark made by him, "Look at so-and-so. Look how fit they are after kids," or, "Go to the gym more, eat more healthy, you're not doing enough." Meanwhile, if I commented that he could also lose some weight, or we should try together, he'd shut me down. "Worry about yourself first."

He was able to trigger all my insecurities and had me begging for his approval, affection, and admiration. I was afraid to lose him. It all felt like one big performance to satisfy him; consistently molding myself to win his adoration. It's interesting that I was questioning myself, while also neglecting my needs. What was he doing to improve on his end? What was he doing to help us get us past this betrayal? I'm the one who changed and exerted myself to save this marriage from the pain that he caused.

I was in my thirties and the biological clock was ticking. On one hand, I thought if we had kids, it would solve our issues. On the off chance it didn't bring us closer, I was prepared to be a single mother. After all, the only reason my ex was pressuring me to try for kids was to fulfill his mom's desire for a grandson. I think, in the end, it was also his desperate attempt to make sure I stayed.

Immediately after sex, I'd feel so strange—an intense repulsion. My body's response was to cry and he'd ask me why I was crying, as if I was a freak. I didn't have an answer for him. Other times, I would run to the bathroom, immediately washing myself because I didn't want to get pregnant with him. I'd sit there in the bathroom crying, knowing deep down having a baby with him was not a good idea.

For one, I knew he didn't quite want a baby. After all, he would say on multiple occasions that his mother and I could raise the child. Aside from this major red flag, I myself felt wrong as a woman, not wanting to bring a child into this world with him. But my body's reaction was an indication of my psyche— I was mentally preparing myself to be a single mother and also scared for my future child. I could not let him be a father to my child. My maternal instincts had unknowingly kicked in and I needed to protect my not-yet-conceived child from this person.

Looking back, I am so grateful I never got pregnant. It was such a blessing. If I had had a baby with him, I would have been stuck in his city, without the support of my family, and would have been berated constantly for my mothering skills. One thing was for sure, I did not like how he made me feel: unworthy, unwanted, broken, and unattractive. Because I know I am beautiful.

I am beautiful because ... I am me, and that's all it takes. My uniqueness is what makes me beautiful. Not the clothes that I wear, not the imperfections I conceal under makeup, not by the way my genetics chose to allocate fat, not the jewelry I adorn myself in, not my skin color, not how I style my hair, not my overgrown eyebrows or the hair that I painstakingly remove. I will not mold myself to meet your limiting perception of beauty. I don't need to play dress-up for my mother-in-law so she can parade around the new bride at the *Gurdwara*. I'm not your show pony. I don't need to compete against girls that my ex compared me to. I am not some video game character he can design and control. My mind, heart, and soul are where my beauty lies. All the parts of me he tried to destroy.

I was still standing—barely. I was tired, but I knew I could make it to the final round. He hadn't been able to knock me out. The thoughts in my head were running a mile a minute:

- You need to endure and accept that this is the way things are—look at all the elder women in your own family
- What about the money that was spent on the wedding?

- My parents will be upset, or they might not support me and tell me to go back to him
- His parents will be devastated (yes, I even thought of his family—my good-girl conditioning still made me try to keep everyone happy)
- It's only been a couple years. I haven't given the marriage a fair shot.
- The grass isn't greener on the other side (according to all the single girl's dating woes.)
- It's not that bad
- What will people say
- It's time to have a baby and if I leave, then that may not happen
- They're just words. He's not hitting you.

This was my brain. I should have quieted it and, just for one second, thought, what about me and my feelings. I was constantly upset, I was sick of feeling like I couldn't do anything right, and I was sick of feeling unloved. I had been so apologetic throughout the relationship, and I had given him chance after chance.

I had convinced myself that divorce was not an option. It seemed unachievable, a foreign concept that had much larger consequences than I was willing to face. I didn't personally know anyone who had been through it.

I expressed all of these reservations to my therapist, and she challenged each one. What I failed to recognize then was that domestic violence doesn't just come in the form of physical violence. Despite him never laying a hand on me, the irony of it all was that I wasn't much different from the women in my family. I endured the violence. I felt helpless. I felt like no matter what action I took, I was on the losing end. That was such a pivotal aha moment. I didn't want to accept what the women in my family had tolerated and accepted for years before me. What about the next time I angered him? What if he couldn't control himself?

I couldn't win the argument with my therapist to support my decision to stay. I knew something had to change. But what? Leaving didn't feel like an option. I felt defeated and stuck. Therapy didn't help me find the magical answer to my problems. I even dragged my husband to therapy with me, since this was an "us" problem. He showed up late and drunk. Afterward, he made me feel stupid for not giving the therapist the "right" responses. He declared that he wouldn't return to therapy, that there was nothing wrong with him or us. He called me mental and told me to continue going to therapy, as I clearly need the help to get my brain right. The brain fog was real. I couldn't think. I couldn't remember anything.

What was I going to do? I never felt so alone in my life. I was desperate for a solution, there was no fight left in me.

Our dog was my saving grace. She was the final straw in me leaving. We got her in the last three months of our marriage—maybe it was our Hail Mary. She came into my life at a horrible time. Little did I know it was also going to be my dog that would give me the support I needed to open up my eyes to what was wrong, to what I was refusing to see.

We really shouldn't have gotten the dog. His mother had told him that she would not allow a dog inside, she was the lawmaker in the house after all. But he was determined to get this particular dog (it couldn't be any other dog). I really wanted to get a dog as well, but I also knew it was best to wait. Our basement was getting some work done, but once it was completed, we would have no problem.

However, my husband was hard-headed and proceeded to put a deposit on the dog. The problems started immediately.

> **Day 1:** We had to arrange the dog pickup. For me, it was a workday and so I asked my husband to make it after work, or over the weekend. He wasn't going to pick up the dog despite being available, instead, he picked

a time that was convenient for his family. So, I had to take my laptop with me and work on the road to pick up our dog.

Day 2: He left for work, leaving me with our dog amidst the busiest time of year at work trying to meet a deadline.

Day 3: Our dog got ill and I had to drop everything and run to the vet. I was already so attached to her. I told my manager about the emergency, but I felt so lousy having known about these timelines before we even got her.

Week 1 and 2: I struggled to take care of our dog solo. I didn't realize how much work puppies were. I had important meetings and at the same time, she needed to be let outside.

Week 3: My mother-in-law returned from vacation and told me she didn't want our dog in the house. She complained about the smell, the dog hair, and the cleanliness of the house as a result. She forced me to take our dog to my rental property, which luckily happened to have a vacant basement suite. I took an air mattress, a few clothes, her things, my work laptop, and moved out.

Week 4: I was happy to have my space and solo time with our dog as my husband was at work. The downside was my husband made me return to my in-law's home every evening to make sure his dad was served his dinner and that I cleaned up after him. I'd finish work, feed our dog, take her for a walk, rush over to my in-laws with her, have dinner and clean up there, then rush back at night to enjoy a couple hours to myself before bedtime. It was exhausting.

On one of these occasions, I had to leave her unattended for one minute as I was leaving my in-law's house. She ended up running around the house, but I didn't think anything of it. I grabbed her and headed back. The next day I got a call from my mother asking me what was going on? She had heard from my mother-in-law that the dog had pooped inside the house on a mat. I knew at that moment I was in for it if my mother had been contacted. It was not the first time my mother-in-law tattled on me to my mom. I had two minutes to breathe before my mother-in-law called. I apologized immediately and genuinely felt horrible about it. I explained the situation and said I would be right over to clean it. She started to berate me. I tried to explain how innocent it was and how I honestly hadn't realized it. I said I'd go buy a new mat right then. She wouldn't let it go and didn't want to do anything, but let it be known that I was a horrible dog mom. I asked her why she felt the need to tell my mother, and her reason was essentially to let my mother know how horrible a job she had done raising me. I asked her if she also told my husband, and sure enough she had. I just didn't get the point of this. She needed two other people to discipline me so she could drive home the message that I was a shitty person, all because my dog shit on the mat.

That was the day I realized nothing was ever going to change. The nagging thought, *I should leave,* and *I can't do this anymore,* had already been ringing in my head for some time. *What am I even fighting for?* Not long after, upon his return from a work trip, I broke the news to him. There wasn't much resistance because his ego just received the ultimate blow and, unlike the times before, he couldn't reel me back in. At that point, his focus shifted to damage control and keeping me away from his family, so I couldn't expose the infidelity.

It was an act of bravery that I dared to challenge everything that I was taught and every deep-rooted belief I held. He, his family, my family, the culture, and society had made me believe I could tolerate the abuse, and that's just the way it will always be. It took me hitting rock bottom to realize I didn't have it in me anymore, I could no longer persevere.

It was sink or swim. I chose bravery and chose to swim against the currents.

You made my vulnerability out to be a weakness, but it was my strength. I just shared it with the wrong person. Showing emotions strengthens bonds. You used my vulnerability against me, leading me to suppress that side of me. You kept knocking me down. I dug deep and found the courage within me to deliver one final blow. I'm walking away a winner.

"If you leave me, you're gonna end up with some loser, living in his basement, watching TV all day. You're never going to do anything fun, travel… just a boring life," said my ex, or, "If you don't like it, there's the door, you can see your way back to your parents."

He challenged me as if I'd be helpless and living a dull life without him. Now I can laugh at these statements while I sit here on a terrace in Spain sipping my café.

Without even realizing it, he led me to make some of my retirement goals a reality in my 30s! In high school, I had studied Spanish and I fell in love with the language. On my travels to Latin America, I discovered that I adore the Latin culture and their pace of life. I decided that I would retire in a Latin country by the ocean and take Spanish lessons.

When I left him, I questioned everything about my life. What would I do now that I fell off the traditional path of life? The unknown was frightening and led me to many anxious moments in therapy. Then I realized, wait, why can't this be my superpower? The brain fog has lifted, and I can see clearly that a marriage is not the end-all, be-all. This divorce was just a chapter in my life, and it liberated me! I was released from the linear path—the parental and societal expectations. And while contemplating life, I realized, I can make some of my dreams happen sooner. There's nothing or no one holding me back. Well, here I am, living out half of my dream in Spain!

Manny is a former corporate professional who left the fast-paced world of North America for a simpler life in Spain, seeking self-discovery and fulfillment. Struggling with marital issues and feeling isolated, Manny found solace in sharing her divorce journey on Instagram, focusing on narcissistic relationships. Her platform aims to empower women to recognize the signs of abuse and take action. Manny now dedicates her time to providing resources, sharing stories, and offering support to those who need someone to talk to by helping them find the courage to leave toxic relationships.

Instagram: @browngirldivorce

https://linktr.ee/browngirldivorce

My Father's Daughter

SHARAN BILAN

I wasn't supposed to succeed. At least, that's what everyone thought. My ex, his family, our community, and even some of my own family expected me to fail. They saw me as weak, not smart enough, and lacking the support I needed to start over. But their doubts became the fuel that ignited my determination.

When my relationship ended, I was left with two young boys and a heart shattered by betrayal. The road ahead seemed daunting, and the whispers of doubt from those around me were almost deafening. They saw a fragile woman, broken by circumstance, and they doubted my ability to rise from the ashes.

But they underestimated the strength of a mother's love. My boys, with their innocent smiles and boundless energy, became my source of inspiration. They helped heal a heart that didn't break. Every laugh, every hug, every moment we shared reminded me of the unconditional love that existed between us. It was through my love for them that I found my own strength.

Until my late twenties, I never felt pressured to get married. I had been in two serious relationships and watched as my friends married one by one. Slowly, I realized that I might be the last one left, and that scared me. It brought back childhood insecurities of not feeling good enough or pretty enough. This fear influenced my relationship with Ravi as we rushed into an engagement.

Our first date was a disaster. Ravi showed up late, acted arrogant, and interrupted me constantly. My gut told me I didn't like him, but I ignored it. I was driven by insecurities, fearing I'd be left behind and believing I wouldn't find anyone better at my age. Ravi looked great on paper, and that seemed enough. One thing stood out. He mentioned his epilepsy. I had no idea how significant that would become over the next five years.

Ravi opened up about his epilepsy on our third date. He didn't hide it, but concealed how he managed it. Diagnosed young, he was on strong medications that made him sleepy and caused early hair loss. My instinct to help and heal kicked in, and I felt protective of him. I researched triggers, holistic treatments, and everything I could to support him. We dated for five months before getting engaged. When I told my father about Ravi's epilepsy, his demeanor changed. He asked if Ravi's family had allowed him to marry me if I had epilepsy. I didn't respond then, but I questioned it throughout our marriage. I already felt inadequate in his family's eyes—not educated enough, not social enough, not religious enough. I wondered if they saw me as acceptable only because Ravi had epilepsy.

When I think back on how all of this shaped me, I also realized that I had no idea how much strength I had inside of me. If someone had told me that I was going to tolerate so much and battle against literally what I knew as my whole world, only to come out empowered, I would not have believed them.

I had lived with my parents my entire life until marriage. As the baby of the family with two older sisters—10 and 8 years older than me—I was admittedly spoiled. Rarely did I cook for myself, and coming and going as I pleased was never an issue since I had been a homebody most of my life. Transitioning to wedded life was an adjustment.

After our wedding on November 25, 2016, Ravi and I moved into his parents' home, which was also shared by his older brother, sister-in-law, and their one-year-old son. This dynamic was challenging, to say the least. It was uncomfortable, awkward, and tense. In hindsight, I see how challenging it must have been for his brother and sister-in-law as well. Adjusting to parenthood is a process, and adding a new sister-in-law and shifting family dynamics only increased the stress. Change is often hard, and all of us had a difficult time acclimating to one another.

The first year of our marriage was a whirlwind. Ravi and I traveled as much as possible and for the first time, we socialized, traveled, and thrived in our newlywed period. We did, however, have conflicting views on spending, budgeting, and family dynamics. Ravi decided to handle our finances early on. I was working at the time and because he seemed so much more money-savvy, I had no problem with this. My check would go into one of our accounts. He would tell me that it was used for our bills, and I asked no questions.

Family dynamics were challenging as well. Living with his family and having essentially three different families under one roof would be difficult for anyone, let alone a mini-family in that home with one spouse suffering from epilepsy. His family felt that I was controlling. My family felt as if I was constantly adhering to him and his family. Often I felt stuck. To avoid conflict, I would relent.

I won't ever say that I was without fault in our relationship because I know that I was the worst version of myself for those five years. I was petty, jealous, out of line at times, and hurtful. I was in pain. At times, when the hurt made me angry, I would say things to Ravi with the intention to hurt him.

Our story was like bouts in the boxing ring—as if we were competing to see who would remain unscathed and for how long.

Still, we decided to keep trying.

When Ravi and I decided to get our own home, it caused a significant rift between him and his family. They blamed me. Ravi's parents had bought a property next door to their home for us. Ravi's father, a general contractor, planned a complete remodel for us. Though it seemed like the decision was solely mine, it wasn't. In fact, Ravi put an offer on the home that would be ours while I was out of town on a girl's trip. He

FaceTimed me from the house and made the offer that day. My name was put on the deed, and I signed all the paperwork for our home with excitement.

Our home was a tract house with three bedrooms and three bathrooms, a small yard, but for me, it was everything. All my newlywed dreams filled that small home with so much love. Ari was born and spent the first two years of his life there, and I spent almost all of my pregnancy with Veer, my younger son, in that home. I lost my dad while living there, and in a way, I lost myself too.

In this new home, we found new problems too.

Among a host of issues was the fact that Ravi turned to alcohol. This created a myriad of breaking points in our already fragile marriage. The funny thing is, I still struggle to call him a full-blown alcoholic – even after being his victim, and going through the battle to set myself free. I still find myself defending the father of my children.

The first incident with Ravi's drinking happened in January at a family friend's party. Ravi got blackout drunk, and his friends carried him into our bedroom at 2 a.m. His mother yelled at them, but she wasn't surprised. Angry, yes, but not surprised. This marked the beginning of many such episodes. Each time followed a pattern: he got drunk, I got angry, he'd promise to stop drinking, and then it would happen again.

His family seemed to blame me for anything that might trigger a seizure, leading to one of the most traumatic events of my life—my firstborn being dropped in the hospital the day after he was born.

Ari was born on September 19, 2018, and his arrival changed me. Motherhood made me want to be a better person in every way. My pregnancy had been challenging, and I had a C-section at 41 weeks. Ravi, despite his epilepsy, was amazing during the surgery. He stayed with me the first night, helping with diaper changes and feeding. The second night, while moving Ari, Ravi had a tremor and dropped him.

It was an accidental, short fall, but it terrified us. I jumped off the bed despite my surgery, checked Ari for injuries, and called the nurses. They assured us he was fine, but I insisted on an MRI, which thankfully came back normal. Ravi asked me not to tell anyone, and I silenced my trauma to protect him.

Ari was a late walker and talker, and I constantly worried if it was due to the fall. But he was a happy baby, bringing joy during dark times, especially after my father passed away when Ari was four months old. When Ari had his first seizure at 18 months, my fears resurfaced. At that time, I was 20 weeks pregnant with Veer, holding Ari in the ambulance, fearing the worst. Ari was diagnosed with febrile seizures, and for almost two years, he was seizure-free. He had another febrile seizure at age four, and then, on his third day of Transitional Kindergarten, I got the call I dreaded. Ari had a seizure at school, not caused by a fever, and was diagnosed with epilepsy. He was prescribed the same medication as his father, bringing my greatest fear to life.

Ravi was eight when he was diagnosed, and Ari was nearly five. I promised myself that Ari would be equipped with the knowledge and tools to understand epilepsy and live his best life.

We would not keep his diagnosis a secret or treat it as something shameful. I also vowed not to enable any behavior because of his epilepsy, ensuring history wouldn't repeat itself.

We would not live in denial and wait for a spouse or partner to find out the extent of his symptoms and condition, like I did.

Ari was four months old when an incident changed how I saw Ravi and the marriage. At that time, I struggled with sleep, breastfeeding, and not being able to produce milk, I had been dealing with PTSD from the fall that he experienced in the hospital, and I had been diagnosed with postpartum depression.

And I faced it alone. Ravi stayed downstairs with his mom, and we told our parents that I had been dealing with a fibroid issue. I was crying, vomiting, shaking, and I remember calling my mom to see if she would bring me toast and tea.

Really, I just wanted someone, anyone to come to me. My mom made some excuse about being busy, but I heard my dad in the background, "I'll go drop it off to her, tell her not to worry." I remember looking out at my dad from the window—and crying even more at the thought of him

knowing about what I had chosen to do. I thought about the fact that three days prior I had called him at midnight, crying "Ravi is really drunk, and he slapped my arm, Dad. HE SLAPPED MY ARM."

I remember my dad's silence. And how much must have been going on in his mind at that statement. He asked me if I was okay, if Ari was okay, and if I wanted him to come get me and Ari right then. I couldn't. I told my dad that I just needed a week. I asked him to please not tell anyone.

And to this day, I think about the fact that I may have been a factor in my dad's death.

There are moments in life that leave an indelible mark on our souls, moments that refuse to fade with time. For me, that moment began on February 2, 2019. A date that will forever live rent-free in my mind. It was the day my entire life changed. The day that would haunt me for the next year and beyond.

My 67-year-old father died of cardiac arrest on that cold February day. He was my greatest confidant, my ally, my friend. The pain of losing him was incomprehensible, a grief so profound that it shook me to my core. He was the only person I had trusted with my deepest secret: that Ravi had hit me, and I wanted to come home. And now, six days later, I was facing the greatest trauma of my life.

My father's death was a devastating blow, a cruel twist of fate that left me grappling with a whirlwind of emotions. The man who had always been there for me, who had been my rock and my protector, was suddenly gone. I felt adrift in a sea of sorrow, struggling to find my footing in a world that had been irrevocably altered. I had asked for a week, and in that week, the parent who gave me strength was gone. Now, how would I find the courage to move forward?

After this, I stayed on. I am not sure why. It was as if, with my dad gone, I found little motivation to live for myself.

My dad was the person in my life who truly saw me. He didn't view me as naïve or silly, and he never judged me for my bad choices. If anything, he would tell me that I never truly saw the potential in myself. He reminded me constantly of how smart, capable, and loving I was. As an only child and a progressive father of three girls, he understood the importance of nurturing our strengths and supporting us unconditionally.

I carry these memories with me every day, the weight of my choices a constant reminder of the pain and loss I've endured. But I also carry the strength my dad showed in his quiet support, a strength that now guides me as I navigate through my life, striving to find peace and healing. His belief in me is something I hold onto tightly, even in the darkest moments.

And when I decided to stay on in that home and that marriage, Ravi's indifference grew to confident arrogance. He was now openly indulging in a lifestyle that seemed geared to diminish my spirit and rub my choices in my face, over and over again.

One trip in particular has become a lasting memory and a rather tight nail in the coffin that was to hold the remnants of our marriage. It was a boy's trip to Scottsdale.

In the days leading up to Ravi's trip to Scottsdale—and the week that would lead to me walking away from our marriage forever—I could sense that something was wrong. He was angrier and more closed off than ever. When I asked him to spend some time with Ari before he left, he quickly turned the request back on me, implying that I thought he was a bad parent. By then, he had become a master of gaslighting. I told my therapist that my memory had become so foggy that I couldn't remember the horrible things Ravi claimed I said about him. His rage would leave me fumbling, questioning what I had really said versus what he accused me of. My depression was at its peak, making me doubt my own worth and capabilities as a mother. I felt immense guilt whenever I needed help from his parents or my mom, believing that I didn't deserve Ari and Veer. They deserved a kind, capable mother—something I no longer felt I was.

"I'm not feeling well. I'm having thoughts about killing myself." I had finally hit rock bottom the morning I called the suicide hotline that appeared on my phone. I was in bed, my hand shaking. Over the past few months of my marriage, I had developed a persistent hand tremor. I initially blamed it on caffeine, but even on days without coffee, the tremor worsened as my anxiety heightened. Ravi stared at me, holding Veer in his arms, while Ari sat in his high chair in the kitchen. As he listened to me on the phone, he showed no concern. No empathy. No compassion. If anything, he looked annoyed as he watched me answer the questions about having knives or guns around, and thoughts of harming others. Answering the questions, I felt my heartbeat slow and my racing thoughts calm.

I looked at Veer, his eyes full of love as he reached out for me. After a few minutes, I hung up. Ravi looked at me, still emotionless. "Are you okay?" he asked. I nodded, and he walked out of the room. I stayed in our room for a few more minutes, and suddenly I heard him shout, "Are you going to do anything today? Can you clean the bathroom?"

Despite knowing his wife and the mother of his children was suicidal, he chose to belittle me instead of helping or understanding. Suicidal thoughts had become a constant. I didn't want to live. I didn't want to exist. To Robby, I felt lazy and unsupportive. To my mother, a constant worry and a problem. To my boys, was I just a lazy and undeserving mother? I isolated myself from friends and family, keeping everyone at arm's length to hide my misery and perceived failure.

Later that day, we took the boys to a playground. Ravi was focused on his phone the entire time, and we barely spoke a word to one another. I took a picture of the four of us with a cheesy quote and posted it on social media, trying to maintain the illusion of a happy family. As long as I looked happy from afar, no one would realize the empty soul I had become.

August 2nd, 2021. The day I left him. The day my life changed forever. I remember it like it was yesterday—the heaviness in my chest as I packed my bags and walked out the door, leaving behind everything I had ever known.

Veer, my sweet baby boy, just one-year-old at the time, would never have the family dynamic I so desperately wanted for him and Ari. My sweet boys, despite their innocence and love, couldn't fill the void that had been growing inside me for years. This void was carved by a marriage that had turned toxic, by a husband who no longer saw me as anything more than a burden to bear.

I had tried so hard to be the woman he wanted me to be, to win back his love and affection. But no amount of weight loss or hair extensions could change the fact that he had stopped loving me long before I had the courage to leave. The ultimate betrayal came when I discovered that Ravi had been cheating on me throughout our entire marriage. It was a blow that knocked the breath out of me, leaving me gasping for air in a sea of lies and deceit. How could I have been so blind? How could I have trusted him with my heart, only to have it shattered into a million irreparable pieces?

As I sat in the doctor's office, waiting for the STD test results that would confirm or deny my worst fears, I couldn't help but wonder how I would ever find the strength to pick up the pieces of my broken life and start again. But deep down, I knew that I had to. For Ari. For Veer. For myself. For the woman I used to be, before I lost myself in the wreckage of a love that was never meant to last.

I realized that leaving Ravi was the most courageous thing I had ever done. It was a leap into the unknown, a terrifying step towards reclaiming my life. The path ahead was daunting, filled with uncertainty and fear, but also with the promise of healing and new beginnings.

My boys became my anchor, their innocent smiles and unconditional love reminding me of the strength I had within. I vowed to create a safe, loving environment for them, one where they would never have to witness the pain and betrayal that had defined my relationship with their father. Slowly, I began to rebuild our lives, finding solace in the small victories and the unwavering support of those who truly cared for us.

As I look back on that day, I am filled with a mix of sorrow and pride. Sorrow for the life and love I had lost, but pride for the strength I found within myself to leave and start anew. August 2nd, 2021 will always be the day my life changed forever—the day I chose to rise from the ashes and reclaim my sense of self, my happiness, and my future.

The days following my departure from Ravi were a haze of disbelief and despair. I had never imagined the crushing isolation that would envelop me like a suffocating blanket, leaving me gasping for air in a world that suddenly felt so empty. I suppose deep down, I clung to the hope that it wasn't truly over between us. That he would fight for our marriage, for the family we had built together, for the promises we had solemnly made to each other on our wedding day. But as the days turned into weeks, and the weeks into months, it became painfully clear that Ravi had no intention of fighting for us.

Looking back, I realize how little I had wanted for myself. How I had allowed my dreams and aspirations to wither and die in the shadow of my marriage and motherhood. I convinced myself that being a wife and mother would bring me all the love and fulfillment I needed in life, but it was a hollow lie that left me feeling more alone than ever.

After Veer's birth, the darkness within me grew even deeper. Thoughts of suicide haunted me, not just in the throes of postpartum depression, but in the quiet moments of despair that followed.

I longed for human connection, for someone to see past the facade I had carefully constructed on social media and recognize the truth behind the perfect photos and glowing captions. But I was too afraid to reach out, too afraid to let anyone in, for fear that they would see me for who I truly was: a broken woman trapped in a loveless marriage.

Ravi's indifference cut me to the core, especially on his birthday, exactly one week after I had left him. I had hoped against hope that he would miss me, that my absence would weigh heavily on him, but his callous words shattered whatever fragile illusions I had left. As he sat in the parking lot of In-N-Out, casually enjoying a meal with Ari, he made it clear that he felt no remorse for what he had done, no desire to reconcile our shattered relationship. Instead, he presented me with a list of demands, a twisted ultimatum that laid bare the depths of his cruelty. At the top of that list was a demand for my silence, my submission to his will, my acquiescence to a life of misery and subservience. And for a fleeting moment, I considered it, for the sake of my children, for the semblance of stability and normalcy they so desperately needed.

But then I remembered who I was, who I had once been before Ravi's toxic influence had stripped me of my dignity and self-worth. And at that moment, I made a choice. To reclaim my life, my autonomy, my voice. It was a choice born out of pain and desperation, but also of resilience and hope. A choice to walk away from the darkness that threatened to consume me and step into the light of a future filled with possibility and promise.

There was still the question of my home, though. What would happen about that property?

Many have asked if I hate him. Given everything that transpired, I did go through a period of hate and heartbreak. But like dealing with a death, I went through stages: denial, anger, sadness. The most significant lesson I learned was that growth hurts. It doesn't come easy. As I healed and grew, I realized only someone hurt and self-loathing would do these things to someone they loved. I believe Ravi loved me in the only way he knew how. I don't waste energy hating him. Instead, I pray for him— pray that he changes for his children and treats the next woman in his life better. I don't need an apology. I simply need him to do better.

The one person who did better for me was my mom. My life came back through my mother – the silent one, the torch-bearer of the ideal Indian family. The one who was scared because now her husband wasn't around to pick up the mantle and do what he always did. Stand by his family and ensure no harm gets in.

My mother and I had always been complete opposites. I was her youngest, the third girl, arriving eight years after my middle sister. We never saw eye to eye on much of anything. I had always been a Daddy's girl through and through. My dad understood me—my humor, my temper. He also adored my mom. No one would have guessed that they had an arranged marriage. They had their fights, but my dad never stayed angry at anyone. It was the quality I loved in him the most. He loved us all so much, and unlike other men of his generation, he didn't shy away from showing it.

As hard as my dad's death was for me and my sisters, I'll never forget my mom's face in the hospital lobby the night he died. I never want to see her look like that again. She looked so small, so scared, and frail, her body shaking. They had been married for 49 years. He was her world. She had already lost both of her parents and two older sisters, and we were all so nervous that this devastation would be too much for her.

My mom was scared when I initially left Ravi. She worried about what kind of life I would have—hardships, being alone. For her, it was the unknown. Getting their daughters married and seeing them live happy lives was what she and my dad envisioned for us. So, coming home and facing my mom was difficult. She wasn't the type to coddle. But I will never be able to thank her enough for what she has given me and the boys in the last few years. Not just a home, but playing the part of mother and father to me.

The first night that I didn't have the boys after leaving Ravi, I was a mess. My mom had me sleep with her. When she heard my silent sobs, she put her arm around me and cried with me. It was the comfort I needed at that time that no one else could have given me. I remember holding my dad's shirt to my chest, finding the solace I needed most.

A year ago, my mother told me she was proud of me for being the mother I was to the boys. It's the first, and only, time I have heard those words from her. Our relationship has changed so much since I left Ravi. We still have our fights and moments, but the respect and unwavering love I have for her now, seeing her play the role of both mother and father, is something I wish I could explain to her. Sometimes, I focus so much on the parents I lost that I forget to appreciate the one I still have. It's something I try to work on every day.

Where do we go from here?

In the following weeks, everything hidden in my marriage came to light. The realization that my marriage was a sham and that my in-laws never saw me as their daughter was one of the hardest things to accept. My father loved deeply, forgiving flaws and embracing those important to him. Despite the challenges with my in-laws, I loved them and thought of them as parents, especially clinging to my relationship with my father-in-law. I yearned for a father figure in my life.

There's a scene in my favorite Hindi movie, *"Kabhi Khushi Kabhie Gham,"* that always made me cry. It speaks of the pain of making a stranger into your family and then having that family member become a stranger again. That's exactly how I felt—discarded like trash, as if I had never been part of their lives for the last five years. There were no calls from them, no visits, nothing. I was simply a picture on their wall that now needed replacing. That hole in my heart might never be fixed, not even with time.

Two years after making that call to the suicide hotline, I would be employed at that very company. I became a manager at the place that had saved my life. Every day, I walked through double doors under a quote on the wall that read, "Everybody deserves to be seen." For someone who had felt unseen for so long, it sometimes brought tears to my eyes. I had the immense honor of working for the unsheltered, unseen, and unheard. They were the underdogs, and in many ways, they felt like kindred spirits.

It's been almost three years since I decided to leave Ravi. I feel like I've died and been reborn—a phoenix rising from the ashes. My confidence has returned. I smile again, and I can look in the mirror without hating the reflection. Most of all, I am proud to be me, something I had never truly felt before. I no longer doubt myself as a mother; it's the one area where I feel I truly thrive.

Sharan Bilan has a diverse background in health administration and a strong focus on nonprofit work. Originally from Yuba City, California, she now lives in Sacramento. As a divorced mother of two lively boys, she enjoys reading and traveling in her spare time. Sharan is also actively involved as a network lead for We Are Saath Northern California, an online platform dedicated to enhancing access to mental health resources within South Asian communities through education, activism, and storytelling. Her mission is to leverage her own experiences and voice to challenge stigmas and reshape narratives around mental health in the South Asian community.

Wed Me

LOVELEEN KAUR

I woke up abruptly. Something was in my throat, and it wanted out. I rushed to the bathroom.

Yack! I aimed the vomit into the toilet, my body in panic mode.

Wait...what did I eat last night?!

"You should take better care of yourself," he casually murmured as he briskly walked away from the bathroom door. A light bulb went up in my head. *You're right,* I murmured. *I need to take better care of myself.* I wiped my mouth, gurgled some water in the sink, and darted back into the bedroom, where Winnie the Pooh with his honey and friends were frolicking on the wall.

I slept the past few nights on the twin bed under Winnie the Pooh, coming back from work to a closed (and sometimes locked) door to our bedroom. In the Randhawa household, closed doors meant "do not disturb."

"What did you say?" He followed me into the room.

"I said you're right, I should take better care of myself. I'm going to the hospital to get myself checked out." I wanted to escape. I wanted to feel safe.

"Yeah, go. You should get yourself checked out." I could sense the smirk on his face.

"You're right. I should get help." I said out loud.

"Yeah, get help. You have a lot of issues. And my parents don't want to deal with this drama anymore."

He was unbearable.

I remembered marriage advice from my *Mohali Massi ji* during our late night chats during wedding week. *Just say yes to everything and then do what you think is right.*

"Are you going to let someone know you are leaving?" he said.

Why did it feel like he was walking me out for good?

"Yeah, I'll let them know after my checkup." I responded.

He was getting furious with every "yes."

"Don't think that you can just come back in and out of the house whenever you like. You should call your parents. You're their problem."

No, I'm not. I clenched my bag. *Just because you are dependent on your parents...* I rushed down the stairs, him following right behind.

'You're just another Bay Area bitch."

He kept hurling hurtful things. For the last three years, I had put up with commentary on my weight gain, my cheap clothes, my athleticism, my vegetarian diet, my love for God and Sikh heritage.

Out of an intense level of frustration, I turned around and threw my middle fingers in the air to the person I vowed "til death do us part." I walked through the garage, looking at my hands, tears down my cheek. *I can't believe I just did that.* As I reached the car door, I looked towards Aman. He was standing in the doorway, already closing the garage behind me.

This was not the first blow-up since our marriage, but this was the last hospital visit before I took off my rose-colored glasses of my fairy tale love marriage. I no longer trusted my husband to uphold the four

Lavaan we took, or the English version we repeated twice, to *take care of each other through sickness and health.* There I was, all alone, feeling bullied to leave the Randhawa house.

What bullshit the idea of marriage became—*there is no us, there's only you, and doing what is best to keep you happy.* Sitting in Urgent Care, I looked at what the doctor prescribed for me after I told her I had recently been traveling and stressed out from having no one to talk to about my failing marriage—it was Zofran and Xanax. I learned that Zofran was a psych drug, as his mom took micro-doses for her chemo treatments. *"I'm prescribed this to deal with my marriage. What has become of my life???"*

Later that day, I drove to San Jose, my parents' disappointed faces playing in my mind. *"What trouble did Bablu get herself into this time?"* But still, I knew my mom's cooking and dad's presence would provide me with enough love to carry on. And they did—for the month I stayed in San Jose, before I went back for another round of a hostile environment Aman had created for me. At least I knew my parents would take me in no matter how broken I would come back the next time.

Within a parent-child relationship in a brown house, we are taught to live up to our parents' expectations. Anything that skews away from their expectations can be considered out of line in what is appropriate behavior. You become engrained to the idea that skewing off the plan even one bit might lead you into a life of worries. I grew up thinking that as long as I focused on my education, earned a master's degree, and married into a Sikh, Jatt family, I would meet the expectations set by my elders, and as an outcome, I would be happy.

I grew up in Santa Clara, California, around a diverse group of minorities and hardworking immigrant families. One of the greatest parenting tips I observed with my parents was to be picky about the neighborhood you lived in for the sake of your children's well-being. Even if that meant a smaller space to afford access to better public-school education. Our family of five lived in a crowded apartment. My siblings and I enjoyed the fruits of my parents' labor. We played outside late into the summer nights, watched 4th of July fireworks visible from Great America, and went to Khalsa School on Sundays at San Jose *Gurdwara*. From Khalsa School, I learned the *Five Pauris of Japji Sahib* that became a staple for centering myself and achieving mental clarity. My parents taught us about *Seva* in the *Gurdwara* and outside, humbly opening their doors to families getting started in America. They also took us along to participate in peaceful protests to bring awareness and stand for social justice for Sikhs in India and America.

From elementary to high school, I was surrounded by beautiful Filipina and Vietnamese girls that had an immense influence on my personal growth. They boosted my confidence, were family-oriented, and believers of God. We went through trials and tribulations as friends— Even though I was *Bablu Tablu* at home—the dark, chubby one— but, with my friends and peers, I learned to embrace my not-so-fair skin tone, curvy body, and creative mind. I learned the importance of respecting myself, found reading, music, and writing to be therapeutic, and loved dancing away worries.

My dad did not drink and did not store alcohol in the house. The only time we saw alcohol in the house was when my dad had a drinking friend over, and even then he would make sure *Chacha ji* was there to drink with them while my dad ate the snacks. My *Chacha ji* was a happy drunk.

By the time I was 23, I had gotten used to a routine of work, gym, school, and home. I started to crave connections with other Punjabi people my age. Something I enjoyed in the community was attending *Akhand Paths,* birthday, and pre-wedding parties at Sneha, the Indian restaurant with the best deals in town. I looked forward to dressing up in Indian suits, eating boat loads of *pakoras*, doing *langar seva* with the aunties and uncles, meditating to hymns and prayers, catching up with cousins, and of course, *bhangra*. I always imagined that I would grow old doing the same things with a Punjabi community of my own to make memories with. However, I didn't personally have many Punjabi friends or knew Punjabi people outside our parents introducing them to me and my siblings. I was afraid of losing the Punjabi dialect, so I decided that I might find like-minded Punjabis if I joined a bhangra team. In middle and high school, I had done bhangra performances and my dad was a bhangra dancer in college. It seemed like a great idea to get back to it.

One day my parents did not tell us where we were headed until we were already on our way to Sneha, to meet *Sweety didi's*, my older sister, soon-to-be husband. I would later learn this was only the second time they were meeting, but by August, we were back in Snehas' for *Sweety didi* and *Jija's roka* where I was the photographer and DJ. By September, they had their court marriage.

A few months later, in-between work, midterms, and bhangra competitions, I flew to India to attend my sister's extravagant wedding in India. It was ten days full of fun festivities, reconnecting with cousins back home in Punjab, and spending time in our childhood home in *Dasuya*. I imagined coming back to India in two to three years for my own wedding. I was less than a year away from completing my Bachelor's degree. Planning ahead, I subconsciously made a decision to pick my own husband before my parents did. Someone that would check their boxes—Sikh, Jatt, and from a humble, hardworking family.

In July that same year, we got the most devastating call from Punjab. My *Darji* was on his motorcycle when he was hit by a school bus and suffered internal bleeding. He passed away before they made it to the hospital. Before leaving the house that day, he made sure to hand over the keys to the house to my *Beeji*. His last wish for her was to eat well and to not wait for his return. This was the first time I dealt with the grief of losing a loved one. He was my father-figure who raised me in his arms when I was little while my dad was in America.

I fell into a pit of despair, grieving the moments I would never get to share with my *Darji*. It hurt to accept that I would never hear his encouraging words and see his beautiful smile again. He was a major advocate in my life to focus on my studies. *Darji* would say, "people can take your house, your jewelry, your clothes, but they can't take your degree from you—they can't take away the knowledge you gain." Constantly hearing this at a young age shaped the way I viewed school. It was very important to get good grades, go to college and one day get a Master's degree.

While my family was in India, attending *Darji's* funeral, I turned to my *bhangra* friends. Social drinking events helped numb the grief. Up to this point, I thought I had a healthy relationship with alcohol. After *Darji* passed, alcohol would trigger sadness, and lead to overindulgence.

I was sitting on the fifth floor of Duncan Hall, zoned out of a Differential Equations lecture, when I randomly got a DM on Instagram from Aman. He asked where I was.

"I'm at school, about to get out soon," I responded quickly.

He was Vice President of the Sikh Student Association at university, and introduced me to the local all-girls bhangra team.

"Cool, are you doing anything afterward? I'm also near campus."

"No, nothing planned." *Besides going back to an empty home,* I thought.

"Okay, let's meet up."

After class, I walked over to Quickly's where we planned to meet. As I approached Quickly's, I noticed a tall, lean man with a sharp nose, and straight teeth. His physical appearance reminded me of my grandpa. I saw it as a sign from above.

We grabbed some bubble milk tea and sat at a table outside.

"Wait, how tall are you?"

"I'm 5'1." *Ugh, another Punjabi person making me self-aware of my height.*

"Dang, really? You don't look like you are. Stand up, let me see."

I stood up.

"Turn around."

I did a little twirl, feeling awkward, but following through the request as they felt harmless.

"Okay, yeah. You are kinda short, but that's okay."

From there, the conversations flowed like water. We delved into his dating life, his big family, his tight-knit circle of friends, and his ambitious plan for a Master's in Accounting.

I shared about my small-knit family, my educational goals, my career in the tech industry and working at WhatsApp.

It was Aman's last summer in San Jose. He was headed back home to live with his parents *nana*, and *nana ji,* about 2 hours away in Bay Area traffic.

We strolled over to the San Jose State campus. Sitting on a bench, he pulled out his EarPods, placing one piece in my ear and one in his, sharing a collection of music he had produced himself. It was a revelation. Here was someone who, like me, possessed a passion for music, but had taken it to another level, crafting his own masterpieces. Even though he would send me samples randomly and ask my opinion, in that moment, I was instantly captivated by his lyrical prowess, his voice, and his production skills. For me, that day marked the beginning of a friendship. Whenever Aman was in town, he'd reach out, and I'd always be there to hang out. We shared endless laughter, danced the nights away, and were vulnerable with each other about our confused Desi lives.

During that first meeting, his questions were geared toward finding out what I was like, and if I would be a good fit for his family. When he told me to spin around, I had no doubts he was looking for a *sidhi-sadhi Jatti* to wife up. A simple girl who wouldn't ask for much, but always be ready to perform her duties to a T. He was mentally checking his parents' requirements using my biodata, but also doing a vibe check. He appeared confident, feminist, calculated, family-oriented—similar to myself.

Although it felt like an interview, it also felt friendly since he shared a lot about himself. With the passing of my grandfather, I was looking for a Punjabi friend with whom I could talk about anything other than the sadness I felt in losing that elderly member of my family. With less time spent drinking to fit in with my bhangra friends, I was very taken in by the fact that I found someone who checked the basic requirements on my parents' list, and that he had so much in common with me. Aman would plan fun dates for us and invite me to any social event he was attending. The more we spent time together, the more I thought the stars were aligned for us to meet.

Within two months, I told him the three little words, "I love you," which caught him by surprise. He didn't feel the same way just yet, and it made me feel like it was something I hadn't earned. Fair enough. As much as I saw myself as *sidhi-sadhi,* it was easy to confuse me for a rebel. After all, I had a huge tattoo on my back and I loved motorcycles. What isn't *sidhi-sadhi* about that? Just like bhangra competitions fulfilled my adrenaline rush, so did motorcycles and secret tattoos.

We struggled as boyfriend and girlfriend, and I confused it for dangerously in love, Beyoncé and Jay-Z energy. Jealousy and chemistry led to arguments and break-ups, as he often wanted to prove that I wasn't *sidhi-sadhi* enough to be presentable to his parents. He talked a big game about helping with the finances for the family hotel, managing a house, taking care of a dog, and making music at home because his parents supported his rap career. He was also transferring to a Master's program at a private school. It was obvious his family was doing well in comparison to my family. We were living in the same area in Santa Clara for the last 16 years. Uber was taking over my Dad's taxi line of work, and I was a broke college student, living from paycheck to paycheck, to then paying school fees. Yet, he had me convinced he was my Prince Charming, and I was about to have my Cinderella moment.

AP Dhillon famously said, *"Eh Munde Pagal Ne Saare, Gallan Wadiyan Wadde Laare, Umar Di Hauli Addiye Tu, Ni Bach Ke Reh."* As soon as I finished my degree, and started looking for a full-time software engineering job, Aman said it was time I introduced him to my family. I warned him, *if I introduce you to them, that means we are bound to get engaged.* He appeared confident that my family was going to love him, just like his family loved me.

When I first showed *Mommy ji* Aman's photo and shared about his background, she was not impressed. She said, *let me know in a couple more months.* Mommy ji is pretty blunt, but a spiritual person. She didn't see stability. When I told Aman my family was not ready, he was pretty upset. "How could they question all this land we have in India... I will get a part-time job or internship while in school..." On the day our families met, *Sneha* was not available. My parents rushed to put a presentable table together at a small, dank Indian restaurant in Sunnyvale. My dad passed one rupee cent to Aman. "It's a tradition in our family," my Dad explained. "When my grandpa got engaged, he too was passed a rupee. We don't believe in dowry, and we are giving you something more valuable than money." It was a beautiful moment of realizing my Dad supported my decision to choose my life partner.

The moments that followed showed Aman in a different light than the low light from a bar lounge or a candlelit dinner. Aman, the accountant, started counting my pennies.

It started with wanting access to my bank accounts even before our engagement. It seemed harmless at first. I thought I was going to learn a thing or two about savings and finances from an accountant. Then, he suggested opening a joint account for shared expenses for the wedding. Even though I happily shared my finances, he used it as a way to track my spending and monitor my income. He could take something as simple as a nearby Target run for a $6 gallon of milk as an example of why I was going to go broke in the future. After marriage, he would ask me to pay up for my share of the hotel costs on family trips, my share of the phone bill, and my share of any meals.

I never had access to Aman's bank accounts, not once. Honestly, I didn't need it. I saw firsthand during marriage that his parents still covered his credit card bills and student loans. He wasted so much time finding deals just to end up spending on new toys or alcohol on a weekly basis. He had been well taken care of his entire life. This made his unsolicited commentary so out of line that priceless moments like proposals, and heirloom items turned into monetized items.

I had started my online research for men's wedding bands to present to him at the engagement party a few months early. I landed on a 14k gold ring with an intricate white gold design on top. I felt spoke to him. A slim band, but bold and unique. When the ring arrived, it was beautiful, and I was impatient to show it to him.

One weekend, Aman, and his family were in the Bay Area doing jewelry shopping for the engagement party. I decided to do a surprise proposal with the ring. I grabbed a big white poster sheet and, in bold letters, wrote a catchy slogan combining our names. I dragged my little brother along for the photo op. While Aman was in store with his family, I pulled up to the parking lot with my brother. As he got out of the store, I called Aman and he answered the phone.

"Hello?"

"Hey, are you still on Mowry?"

"Yeah, I'm at the jewelry store, like I told you. We liked some sets, but will probably check other stores out..." I waited for the signal. "Wait... is that your car?" My Sonata had enough custom touches to stand out.

My brother and I both popped up from behind the car, the poster opened in my hand, camera in my brothers. The family stared stunned as they tried to make out the words on the poster. I decided to read it out loud so they would catch the puns.

Once everyone was caught up, we all laughed a bit, and I passed the ring to Aman. He looked at the ring, and said, "Wow, when did you get this?" I think he was concerned he hadn't noticed any large expenses on my cards. He passed it around. Everyone took a brisk look and commented on the unique design. We got together and took some pictures to commemorate the moment. It seemed Aman loved the reaction of the crowd. Little did I know that at the end of the marriage, I would hear, "It's *just from* Kay Jewelers."

As we got closer to the engagement day, Aman kept asking if he was going to get a bigger ring presented at the party. He wanted to make sure it was heavy, like the one his Grandpa had. These conversations were always awkward for me. Yes, my parents had plans to buy a ring to give to Aman, but I was afraid of my parents finding out that Aman had specific requests. The day we were shopping around for rings, I made the mistake of letting Aman know. I asked him what he wanted. He said he wanted a 18k gold ring with diamonds.

As I was browsing the jewelry store with my parents, I guided my parents towards a rectangular 18k gold ring with nine little diamonds. I knew they were buying it in hopes to avoid any tension. While we were getting it resized, one of the diamonds popped out. When I sent him a photo of the ring, I did mention that the ring had been left at the shop to get the diamond fixed because it looked like it was going to pop out. From having been that transparent about the situation, Aman spoke back angrily, "Wow, you guys couldn't even find a nice ring that didn't have diamonds popping off? Only if the diamonds are small would they pop off. If it's not even the best ring, then why'd you pick it? Do you know how much I spent on your ring?" That night, I cried a lot. I was reminded that I put myself in this situation and I have to make the best of it. I swallowed every desire to call this wedding off, convinced that maybe I had not spent enough of my own money (since he was watching my bank accounts) to show Aman how much I loved him too. I used some of my personal savings to buy another diamond ring; this time the diamonds were even bigger and given the size of the ring, you'd think the man won an NBA championship.

Scared to feel my own feelings, I just ignored the red flags. Had I listened to myself on how outrageous the whole thing was, I would have called it off. I decided to balance my emotions while pleasing the wants of others. Not concerned about my own.

I did not have much time to get into the real issues. The wedding cards were already out. There was an entire wedding that had been planned. I was not sleeping much, and my levels of excitement and anxiety were both high. On the day of the wedding, I woke up after a sleepless night. Still, I was ready by 9 a.m. and even had time to take care of work emergencies. Throughout the festivities, though, what I realized was that we spent our whole engagement planning for this day and never talked about the rest of the future ahead.

There were 350 guests at my wedding, but none of my friends I grew up with got an invitation. Not even my childhood friend, Felicia, that I dreamed a million times of witnessing my crazy, fat Indian wedding. The financial reasoning from Aman was that there was no space for my friends in the guest list, since the priority was to accommodate his extended family. He also pointed to the fact that my best friend gifted us a Welcome mat for the house which read, 'The Randhawas.' He claimed she got it so people could step on their family name.

In reality, my friend was a thoughtful gift-giver, getting a mat that looks like a cassette tape, tapping into Aman's interest in making mixtapes and producing music.

But of course, his parents supported his rationality. At a point of weakness, he next claimed to the parents that my friends smoked weed, so it was better to cut them off now. The same guy that would later sneak around his house, smoking weed while his parents were asleep, begging me to smoke weed with him to enhance his pleasures and be high during intimacy.

There were two things I wanted during the wedding—to get married at the auspicious time and keeping my last name as *Kaur*. The *Laavan* was supposed to happen at 11 a.m., as we believe the auspicious start to marriage is early in the day. My family had originally booked Fremont Gurdwara to save time on Bay Area traffic, but Aman wanted the San Jose Gurdwara because it was the bigger Gurdwara, so it took additional travel time. They did not show up on time.

Keeping my last name as *Kaur* was the other thing I was attached to. I was proud to be a Sikh, and as a feminist, I wanted to be treated equally to any man. I thought my spirituality was attractive to Aman, but not in comparison to his ego. We both knew our family history, there was no need to announce to the world that I come from a Jatt family just like his or that I now was a part of his family.

Those wishes were not granted. After the wedding ceremony, I had to change my name or else Aman would not sign the marriage license. I couldn't believe obtaining the license was not on anyone's radar, and the Randhawas seemed to think it was funny, calling the situation a "trial of marriage." I did not think it was funny. I was on my toes, making sure I didn't upset Aman from signing the license. Yet, the license never stopped him from throwing the dreaded "D" word if there were disagreements—*divorce*. There were times when he never answered his phone, when he didn't come home for hours after work. "Ask my mom, she knows where I was," he'd say.

This was the first six months of our marriage.

It didn't get any better over time. A year of commuting two hours back and forth from Modesto to San Jose, I landed a job with the City of Modesto IT Department and happened to be assigned to the Police Department. When I got home and told the family about my first day,

Aman began to ignore me in the house for two weeks, and I couldn't get a word out of him as to why. I knew something about my new job wasn't sitting well with him. After a glass of wine or two, he revealed he had been picturing me talking with male officers at work all day, and he didn't like the idea of me talking to other men. There was so much wrong with this behavior, it showed his lack of trust in me, and lack of understanding how hard I work at establishing my skills and career in IT, and still not be given the same respect as male engineers.

This relationship made me realize one of my love languages—*words of affirmation*. Aman was someone I truly loved, but his words, and sometimes lack of words, cut like a sword.

Sometimes I questioned if he thought I was dumb and naive. He hid and blocked me from Instagram on his own personal account, but continued to log into a shared Instagram account with me, pretending he had no interest in social media (i.e. shared password and he had to approve what I posted on it since, by his logic, it was his account too). He would be snooping around my girlfriends' profiles with his personal account, the same friends he claimed to be bad people.

As these silent treatments continued, I began to find that I was in a space where I did not feel comfortable or safe with him. I instantly got the feeling that I was at someone's whims at all times. It began to feel like I was not allowed to have a life outside the home, where I catered to the in-laws.

Even finances were being used as a weapon to make me more submissive to their so-called rules. I could not believe it when he purchased a car for his dad on the week of my birthday. The whole week, as he was searching around for the right deal, he ignored my calls and texts questioning where he was after work. He would not give me clear answers, and eventually started with the cold shoulder, threatening to hit me "accidentally" with muscle spasms in his arm to my face. Then, he showed up on Friday night with a brand-new Camry.

Although I thought the gesture to buy his dad a car was sweet and inspiring, I did not see it as a feasible financial decision to make when he was $40,000+ in school loan debt and currently making payments on his own car. He was working part-time on campus, and not contributing anything to our joint bank account.

I did not expect him to contribute, either. I understood that he was a college student and his parents were involved with his finances. I tried offering to start making payments towards his loan so that we could start making plans to buy a home closer to tech jobs in the Bay Area. I thought marrying an accountant would mean that I would develop good financial habits and have someone to learn from, but it felt more like he had calculated that marrying me would mean additional income for his family's expenditure, while he focused on building his own wealth.

This all took a toll on me. I felt so distant from my family and friends. I did not know who I could vent to about living with a husband who forced you to become a Randhawa on paper, but tells you that you are not one of them. During the month I was home in San Jose, some friends noticed my more frequent appearances on social media. Some saw it as a cry for help.

They knew Aman read my conversations, and so they waited for opportunities to ask me in person at the *Gurdwara*, at events I all of a sudden started appearing at (but would immediately start crying after seeing people I had not seen in 3–4 years), if I was safe. When I went back to the Modesto house after a month-long stay in San Jose, it was starting to become Me versus Them. If I asked to paint the white walls in our bedroom, they said it would bring down the value of the house (the rest of the house was colorful, just not our bedroom). Were we moving? Was that why the market value mattered? If I said I found a good real estate deal, they said it was bad luck to have the number 13 in the house number. I said, "But your house number is 2132…" There was no rebuttal to the theory, and I could tell, nobody was liking my response. At one point, Aman's mom applied for a job at my workplace without even mentioning it to me. It was so strange that they purposely did not want to let me know, despite us living in the same house.

At this point, Aman opened up to the idea of moving closer to the Bay Area. He compromised on an apartment 20 minutes away from his parents' home. He claimed we should make this move in order for him to step up and take better care of our finances. In hindsight, I realized this was just a way to separate me from the family, so that I would not continue to bring up "issues in our relationship for them to solve." His parents and grandpa were always ready to let me know that I was out of line for speaking up because I was the woman in the relationship. To them, I was the real issue.

The real issues began to gain structure in my mind. I realized that they were uncomfortable with the idea of me making more money than him. He even acknowledged and mentioned this to me. To safeguard the peace at home, I turned down job offers and limited my own success. I would have anxiety every time I got a job offer and the salary was double his, fearful of retaliation. Yet, when I didn't take those offers, he would compare my salary to that of doctors and dentists in the family, forgetting the debt-free and humble beginnings I come from. The irony is that I found out he had not even gotten his Master's degree. He had lied about graduating. I found this out during the divorce proceedings and some digging on the college website, where his name was missing from the graduating students list. That's possibly why he always felt wounded when I would do well.

Instead of questioning why things were this way, and regardless of whether I was okay with it, I began to pander to their mindless, flimsy, egos to pay them back for providing me food and shelter, because me showing up and participating as a family member was never enough.

At his house, I was expected to prioritize their events, family, and friends. My environment had completely changed when I got married; no longer surrounded by my own family members and friends who loved and inspired me.

When Aman and I moved out to the apartment, I had my first girl's day outing with *Sweety Didi* and my best friend, Felicia. Before the luncheon, *Sweety Didi* would stop by the Modesto house occasionally to "see" me on her way home from work (a wellness check). Felicia's dad passed away earlier that year, and I still hadn't made it out to see her in the Bay Area. Instead, she drove to the Central Valley to come see me. The three of us needed a journey down our memories as innocent neighborhood kids, growing up together, and appreciating the simple life.

I went back to the apartment after lunch, only to be greeted by Aman, questioning what we did for the girls' lunch. I brought up the fact that I had spoken to the girls about things that had been bothering me. I had been holding back information for over a week because we had just celebrated our three-year anniversary last weekend, and I did not want to ruin my chances of seeing *Sweety Didi* and Felicia. I mentioned the fact that I had put an audio recorder by the door to see if and when maintenance stopped by. This was the same day Aman decided to work from home and wait for the maintenance. When I got home that day, I turned off the audio recorder and didn't play it because Aman confirmed he had been home during the maintenance window. A few days later, when I went to delete it, I forwarded the audio to the part where I heard the door close after I left the apartment. Aman was in the shower. A few minutes into letting the recording play, I heard a bunch of clicking of a mouse, then a girl moaning, from what sounded like the living room TV. The moaning continued, and then the sound of a flush. I deleted the audio. I was hurt. The night before, he had rejected any intimacy and said he was not in the mood. Now he was getting off to porn! Sex was on his accord, not when I was in the mood.

My sister found me in the apartment bedroom, collapsed on the ground, exhausted from the anxiety of being around someone who felt unsafe. She picked me up and brought me to the kitchen and asked what had happened.

I questioned whether he even felt a connection with me. Instead of answering my question, he flew off the handle and got angry about being questioned and recorded. I shared with him that in the same recording, I heard the conversation he had with his brother. On the phone, he was convincing his brother he did not know if I attended my work conference. This was the first conference and only conference I went to. The same work conference where I paid for his flight so he could join me. The same conference where I had catered to his every whim, at all times. So you can imagine how bad it felt that he was misleading his family.

No amount of tears down my face or hurt in my voice softened his heart. He began to pack his bag, and threatened to tell his parents that I had "recordings" of him. When I asked him why he was defensive over his actions, he pinned me on the bed and pierced my heart with his angry eyes. I pushed him off and rolled up in a ball next to the bed. "You're going to regret this," he kept saying. Now, his lack of affection made so much sense.

He left and didn't come back that night.

I waited until the next day before I went to my parents' home. By the end of the weekend, he had transferred his money out of the joint account. I came back to the apartment that Sunday and noticed bottles missing.

The following Monday, his mother called to ask me if I knew where he was. That is when I began to see a pattern. He would pick up alcohol at the apartment and disappear. I wouldn't hear from him and had no idea what was going on.

He began to track my location. I did not feel safe. Especially because he left quite aggressively. I cannot forget how he had purposely kicked me in that same apartment and claimed that he did it involuntarily by mistake. I knew I was not safe even though he had left.

Alone in that apartment, there were mornings when I got out of bed, but my knees shot to the ground. I had never been so uncontrollable in my own body. I'd cry while I texted my coworker, "I'm not able to come in again, I'm not feeling well." I imagined my teammates discussing my odd attendance more and more.

I took walks, long walks in the neighborhood. I went back to doing Japji Sahib in the morning before work. It helped to calm my anxiety back down to levels that were controllable. I was regaining mental clarity on the life I wanted to live. My friends came to see me, they left me plants and books to nourish with. I regained strength at my work gym, comfortable knowing Aman could not be there. When I stayed at the apartment on weekends, my Bhabhi ji would call me and sometimes drive herself over, pick me up, and force-feed me to make sure I ate. Bit by bit, I had an appetite to eat again, and a desire to live longer.

One day, I got a call from his cousins. He had been out in San Francisco, at the bars, hanging out with random girls, accompanied by his little brother Raj.

"How do you know it was Aman?" *my heart was pounding loud.*

"We saw it all… In the Snapchat video… Raj didn't realize he shared it with us."

"But it was him??"

"Yeah, we could see him in the video, even though Raj quickly panned the bar."

There was silence. *My heart sank. It's over. I can't do this. He's embarrassing me.*

"I knew it."

"Girl, you deserve better than this. I know it sucks to hear, but I wanted to be honest with you about what I saw, since you're just sitting alone in that apartment, thinking he's at home with his parents."

The next day, I called his parents and said I needed to collect my Punjabi suits and jewelry from their home because I wanted to attend family events at the *Gurdwara*. They said they were not available, and so I could not come to the house. Vaguely, they said they will let me know when I can stop by and collect my belongings. I waited for three or four days before taking control of the situation.

My co-workers from the Police Department were beginning to pick up on my absences; in the mornings I would call in sick because I would collapse from anxiety as soon as I would wake up, fearful of the world outside. I wanted no part of what was going on, and I wanted to extract myself and my family from all of this. So I asked my good friend Cindy how I could possibly have an officer escort me to get my belongings from my in-laws' home. It was an awkward and hard conversation to have, but I felt safe speaking with them.

The staff at Modesto Police Department allowed me to excel, gave me a safe space to be myself—they were tech-savvy, seeking justice for all, and family-oriented people. My coworkers willingly dove into a dumpster to retrieve my phone when I was moving out of the apartment. I felt the support of my community.

On the day I went to pick up my belongings from Aman's parents' home, the Randhawas were home, but pretended not to be. So, the officer banged the door louder for them to hear. They finally opened the door.

Aman was running up the stairs, yelling at his parents, "She's trying to get me arrested! She's going to file a domestic violence case against me and have me arrested! Why'd you open the door?!" He was running around like a headless chicken.

The police quietly ignored him, explained the civil complaint process, and asked me to start taking my belongings. As I walked upstairs, I saw that Aman's mom had already started packing my belongings out of the bathroom and closet. I headed to our bedroom at one point, with Aman following closely behind, saying, "Your things aren't here."

I went into the room nevertheless and picked up the photos of my nieces, scraps of jewelry pieces, and my documents. I collected pictures, clothes, passport, and jewelry from the Winnie the Pooh room, leaving behind what I couldn't carry out in 10 minutes. I threw everything I could into the back of the car. As I made my last round, I remembered my wedding heirloom from my grandparents, the precious *chandi di garvi,* a pure silver vessel. I asked Aman's mom if she could bring it down for me. At first, she pretended she did not know what it was and where it was. She even commented, "I'll return it to your mom with the jewelry. It's not yours." His mom then asked, "Do you want your wedding dress too?" Woman to woman, that hurt a lot. But I decided to not get entangled further. "Yes, go ahead. Bring me that too." As Aman's mom brought my bright red wedding *lengha* down, I placed the house at the bottom of the staircase, willingly agreeing to never come back.

That is how I left my marital home.

That is how my marriage ended.

The reason my story is called 'WedMe' is because the entire wedding came from my wedding planning app idea—something that I was trying to pursue when I was getting married. While my ex had been very supportive about the app and my idea before we got married, he began to criticize it after we married. Without any support and watching him pursue other app ideas with other people, I dropped the ball on that.

Now, I have picked up the app idea again—but in a different direction. It is less about the planning for the event and more about helping couples start their lives in the best way possible, with open communication and compatibility.

He may have WedMe, but the marriage did not last. And I want couples coming to the app to last the whole length of their lives, with a healthy relationship as their bottom line and key takeaway from the app.

Loveleen Kaur is the founder and President of Leen Tech, a software development and IT consulting firm focused on customer-centric solutions. WedMe is a relationship development tool built by Leen Tech. Loveleen was born in the rich tapestry of Punjab, India, but grew up in the 90s in a humble two-bedroom apartment, alongside her two siblings and parents in Santa Clara, California, USA. A family-oriented, spiritual, and self-motivated leader, she is driven in the principles of *Vand Shakna, Keerath Karni, Naam Japna* – sharing, earning, and remembering God – Loveleen developed a profound sense of purpose and a commitment to serving her local community by working in local government and mentoring young immigrants on college applications in the U.S., job seeking, and managing finances. Since filing for divorce in 2019, Loveleen completed her childhood goal of achieving an MBA degree. This unique blend of Sikh heritage, and American upbringing has fueled her passion for empowering small businesses through technology.

The Red Dress

DEEPIKA SANDHU

I didn't wear red to my wedding.

I thought it was too bold. Too showy. Not me at all.

But today I am in red.

A striking, form-fitting, full-length gown in bright tomato red with a thigh-high slit and ruffles.

Makeup done. Hair done. High heels on my feet and big square gold earrings dangling from my ears.

I am ready to walk the red carpet.

Ready to fully own every inch of my story that got me to this point.

Yet there was a part of me, even in this triumphant moment, that was having trouble believing this was true.

I never imagined wearing a dress like this.

I never imagined wearing a color like this.

But then again, I didn't imagine many of the circumstances that ended up playing out in my life.

I certainly never imagined that my life would end up the subject of a book, for which I was about to win my third literary award.

But here I am.

It is a far cry from where I once was.

A loveless marriage. A painful divorce. A dismantling of everything I knew and thought I wanted. I spent so many years trying to create a life that seemed perfect from the outside. A happy family. A beautiful house. Nice cars. Fabulous vacations. Lots of smiles posted on social media for all to see. Now that perfectly curated life was gone. Burnt up in an inferno of lengthy divorce proceedings, lies, arguments, trickery, pain, shame, anger, frustration and brutal sadness.

I didn't see it playing out like it did.

I didn't know that the ending of one life in a courtroom would be the start of another where I was beaming on the red carpet camera, lights flashing in my direction.

Back then, all I knew is that I needed to say no to the life I was living.

If you call sobbing in your closet living, that is.

I was doing the ugly cry. Wearing my old tattered jammies, my face buried in a pillow so no one could hear me, curled up on the floor, snot running down my face, full body heaving type of cry.

Why was it all turning out like this?

Why, if I had done everything right, was everything feeling so wrong?

Was I just ungrateful for this life?

I have what most people are searching for. The handsome husband. The cute kid. The nice house. The fabulous vacations. Loads of smiles posted on social media for all to see.

Why wasn't this enough for me?

Isn't this what I was searching for back in my twenties?

Back then, I dated like it was a professional sport. I had a long, detailed checklist of the kind of man I was looking for, and I was relentless in the pursuit of that man. If a guy I went on a date with didn't have one of the items on my checklist, I ended it right then and there. In fact, I often ended it far before it needed to end because I never wanted to get dumped. I was far more in control if I was the dumper.

My parents were doing their part too. Introducing me to potential men all the time.

You know, Mr. Singh. Well, his uncle's brother's cousin has a son and he sounds perfect.

Does he really, Mom?

He is a doctor and his father was a General in the Indian army.

That's why he sounds fabulous?

I gave him your number so he will be calling. Be nice and don't scare this one away!

Scaring men away was apparently something I was particularly good at. I didn't even know I had this talent until I started to exclusively date Indian men in the hopes of finding my future husband. I am not speaking for all Indian men, but I am speaking for the hundred-plus first dates (yes, really) that I went on in my late twenties and early thirties, and I am pretty sure I scared more than ninety of them away. I was confident. I had a Master's degree. I was successful. I made good money.

Then I met Vikrant.

Vikrant was the last in a long string of men I met from the website IndianDating.com. He wasn't the last because I eventually married him, he was the last because after another lackluster first date, I declared to my sister, who was also my roommate at the time, that my next night would be my last first date, at least for a while. Preferably, a long while.

I just can't do it anymore, I announced to my sister. I tossed my purse, plopped down on the sofa, and sighed. Tonight's date had a lazy eye. A key detail conveniently missing from his online dating profile.

I am getting the wine, she said, as she got up from her law books.

I am taking a break, I declared as my sister joined me on the sofa, two glasses of wine in hand.

You totally should, she said in her always supportive you-go-girl kind of way.

It's exhausting to put yourself out there time and time again.

Agreed. Take a break. You will find the one. It will happen when you are not looking.

What does that mean? I say exasperated. *When you are single, you are always looking!*

I don't know what it means, but everyone says it, my sister says with a smile. *Just look less actively, at least for a while.*

We drank to that. Not just the glass, but the entire bottle.

The next day, I reluctantly went out with Vikrant. It was the last scheduled date, and then I would be free to leave this dating circus behind. Not forever. But for some time until I could handle the ruckus again.

Vikrant wasn't the man of my dreams. Far from it. My dreams were clouded by the over-the-top cinematic wonders of Bollywood. Bollywood had me believing I would be singing *Hindi* love songs in the Swiss Alps in a chiffon *sari* while my tall, fair, handsome leading man swooned over my slender hips, gyrating to the beat, mesmerized by my long, lush, black mane whipping in the wind. Never mind the fact that my hips aren't slender, I have never been to Switzerland, and I am pretty sure if I did manage to get myself to the top of the Swiss Alps, I would freeze in a chiffon *sari*. Oh, and I can't sing, especially not in *Hindi*. I did say it was a dream, right?

But who was my dream man? After so many dates with so many Mr. Wrongs, and Mr. Not Rights, I was starting to question if anything on my checklist was worth hanging on to. Even more than trying to check the boxes of my dream man, I was tired of being rejected. Of being passed up. Over and over again. As much as I was dating like a professional sport, I was also letting myself go on dates with men that I knew were not good enough or right for me in any way. All in the hopes that maybe I was wrong about what external qualities, traits and attributes my Mr. Right would have. There was always a part of me that thought maybe I just needed to fit a square peg in a round hole? Maybe I was being too picky? Maybe I needed to settle for something different than I desired?

Friend after friend was getting married. Attending bridal showers and bachelorette parties became a normal weekend activity. The conversations at these events were always the same.

Are you seeing anyone?

Are you still single?

Oh my gooooooddddddddd, I can't wait until you find someone, and we are doing this at your wedding!

Those questions were usually followed by sarcastic giggles and the follow-up question of *"How old are you now?"* A not so subtle reminder that time was ticking away. My marriageability as an Indian female was decreasing day by day, year by year.

All of this was in the backdrop as I approached the Mexican restaurant where Vikrant and I had agreed to meet. He texted, "Be there in five." I was already there, punctual to a fault, standing outside the restaurant.

I texted my sister, *"I hate going on dates."*

She replied instantly. *"I know. Last one. Just have fun."*

As I was texting back a witty reply to my sister, I heard two long honks of a horn. In a completely quiet part of town, the noise startled me. I looked up from my phone and an Indian guy in a pristine white Lexus pulled up across the street from the restaurant and was honking at me. It was him.

Oh, hell no. I am not seriously about to go on a date with a guy who just honked at me. Like, what the hell! This is about to be worse than Mr. Lazy Eye.

There was a part of me that wanted to run away right there. Is this really the kind of guy I am meeting? One who thinks it is perfectly okay in 2007 to honk at someone on the street? And am I the kind of girl who would ever in a million years go out with a guy who honks at a girl? Me? The last time a guy honked at me, I was 21 years old, on vacation in Chandigarh, walking with my *Masi* in Sector 17. At least that guy blew a kiss as he honked and sped by.

It took everything in my power to stay there.

But, what choice did I have?

I was not 21 anymore.

Could I afford to let another guy walk out of my life?

Was I going to let another guy go by the wayside because he didn't meet my checklist, wasn't up to my standards?

Did I have that luxury anymore?

Did I have that kind of time?

If I wanted to have my Indian fairy tale wedding, if I wanted to be a mom and have a family, if I wanted to make my parent's dreams of watching their firstborn get married, and if I wanted to zip the lips of the noisy aunty brigade that was busy gossiping at every party that my marriage was getting late, well then, I had to stay. I had to make it work.

And I did.

Not just that night on that date.

But date after date, after date.

I kept trying to make it work.

Even when I knew in my gut that this wasn't it.

I kept trying to make it work.

After all, he had potential.

Fun-loving, handsome, intriguing eyes, large circle of friends, always the life of the party, decent job. He seemed like he wanted to stick around with me too. Always doing just barely enough to keep me. Not calling for days, but then having a long chat about something mundane. Not making plans to meet again, but then calling and saying he was driving by, and inviting himself over. It was some version of bread crumbing before that term appeared in the Urban Dictionary. Plus, he didn't have a lazy eye. That alone made him better.

I decided that these lackadaisical building blocks could contort into a marriage. I was going to make this work. No, I didn't love him. No, I didn't even like him on most days. There wasn't any desire. There wasn't passion. There wasn't even a longing to be with him or even a sensation of missing him when he wasn't around. But he was good enough. A possible version of happily ever after might exist with him if I stuck with it. So I did. Through every bad date. Every time he missed something important for me. Every time he didn't introduce me as his girlfriend. Every party where he gave his friends far more attention and importance than he gave me. All the times I went home in tears, I still stuck with it.

It was my decision alone. No one forced me into this one. Least of all my mom. She wasn't happy because he was from India with a different set of cultural expectations, a different background, and not as accomplished as me. *"I just want you girls to find men worthy of the women that you two are,"* my Mom would always say to my sister and I.

But I decided I wasn't worthy of the worthiness my mother sought for me.

I had to settle.

I had to give in.

I had to play small.

So I did.

Time and time again.

It wasn't always bad. But it was never good either.

It was never the feeling of being lit up from the inside. The feeling of being supported, of being desired, of being in a true partnership. It was never the feeling of love. Our life always felt as if it was for show. It looked so good on the outside. While we dated, while we were engaged, while we were married. But it never felt good on the inside.

My family knew it. My friends knew it too. There were numerous times when my family and friends tried to make sure I saw what they were seeing. Take the time one of my oldest and dearest friends, Miriam, came to town. She was visiting from Los Angeles and her trip happened to coincide with one of the many off-again dating periods with Vikrant. My sister, Miriam, and I wore our cutest sundresses, grabbed our wide-brimmed floppy hats and decided to head out to Napa for the day. It was a quintessential California day. Bright blue sky, the perfect number of pearly white clouds masking just a bit of the sun's warmth. Soon we would be sipping wine and frolicking in the gorgeous vineyards. On the one-hour drive, our conversation went in every direction from politics, to clothes, to makeup and eventually love. My friend wanted to know what was happening between me and Vikrant. She clearly did not like what she was hearing about him. For many months, I was giving her the full play-by-play on the relationship. She knew the good parts but got much larger doses of the bad parts, since let's face it, there was more of that to share.

On the drive she asked me, "But Deepika, do you love him?" Without hesitation, I replied, "In our culture, we don't have to marry for love." I could see the disappointment in her face. I knew the sadness she felt watching a friend deflate her own dreams trying to make a relationship work. She had seen me through my dating life, in and out of different relationships, and she knew how much I wanted love to be the center of any relationship. At least until now. But I also knew that I just used culture as yet another excuse for playing small.

What my friends and family didn't know is that I saw it all too clearly but willfully, totally and completely decided to stay in it anyway.

While dating, in marriage, through every up and down in our lives, I was continuously playing small. Dinner parties with his friends crystallized this every single time. The only way I survived these evenings was by having at least two cocktails. Back then, I believed that I was the unfriendly one. It was my demeanor that made his friends not like me. Maybe a drink would loosen me up, help me find their talk more interesting, and somehow make myself more palatable to them. One night that almost worked. I was tipsy, which meant I suddenly became willing to engage in meaningless chatter. One of his friends asked me, "So, what are you working on these days?" I confidently replied, "I am writing a book, and you all are going to say you knew me one day." The friends roared with laughter.

"You are NOT writing a book!" they exclaimed.

"Do you know how hard that is? Not anyone can just set off and write a book!"

"Oh, we will say we knew you one day, how can that be?"

My favorite comment from that night was, *"Vikrant, do you even hear what your wife is saying? She plans to be famous over a book she will write. What will you do then?"*

The banter was in full force. They started making fun of Vikrant for having a wife who was going to be famous for a book. He participated in the banter too. He started laughing hysterically, pretending to be a tiny shop owner in an Indian market, where he would have a stall selling my books and charge extra if I signed them.

Joke after joke ensued. But what they felt was mindless banter hit me as insults. I just stood there faking a smile, trying not to feel hurt. Knowing this is just what they all did when they were together. But there was a piercing sensation that with each taunt, each line, each time they all roared with laughter, they were diminishing who I was, what I was capable of, what I knew in my heart I was meant to do and who I was meant to become.

But that wasn't the worst part. Vikrant was not only letting them mock me, but he was piling on his own mockery too. From their perspective it was all in good fun, a little harmless banter. No big deal. To me, it was a dagger.

If my friends or family had ever made comments like that to him, I shut them down, diverted the conversation. Why? I was always making choice after choice that he would be happy, that he gets to do what he likes, that he feels important, that his voice be heard. But as I did, mine got smaller and smaller and smaller. I suppose it was easier that way. Far easier, than trying to be supported in the way I desired to be supported. Cared for in the way I desired to be cared for. Loved in the way I desired to be loved. Sure, we discussed it. Sometimes we fought about it too. He might change for a few days or a few months. But life went back into a perpetual hamster wheel of just doing the same things each and every day, just playing house, administering life and continuously accepting less.

For seven plus years I let this persist. Until I couldn't any longer.

I was suffocating in this life. I was losing myself, becoming unrecognizable in a life I chose to be in. But this version of me that I was becoming to stay in this marriage was not one I wanted to be any longer. I didn't want to be fighting with him. I didn't want to defend him to my friends and family. I didn't want to have to leave my accomplishments and my successes at the door and put on a fake costume every time I entered my home because I knew he wouldn't understand or be supportive of all that I was becoming at work. I didn't want to tiptoe around my own home wondering when he would be happy, when he would be upset. I didn't want to be under one roof but living two completely separate lives. I didn't want to live in a home where even our habits and interests were so divergent that even the small commonalities that once existed fizzled away.

We were incompatible in every way.

Without a foundation of love for each other, there was nothing for this marriage to survive on. I couldn't do it for others. I couldn't even do it for my daughter. The thought of being in this home, living in this way—cold, uninterested, uninspired, unloved, and undesired—seemed a death sentence I was unwilling to administer to myself.

Sobbing in my closet, seven years into this marriage, I made a decision.

No more accepting less.

No more diminishing myself.

No more doing it all for show.

I wanted a life that lit me up from the inside and was extraordinary in every way. Not in material possessions. I had plenty of those already. I craved, long for, desired extraordinary in every cell of my body. To wake up each day inspired, excited, full of love, ready to take on the day.

Not slamming the snooze button, burying my head back in the pillow, unable to face the day.

I was sick of complaining to girlfriends about my marriage. I was sick of drowning my sorrows in another cocktail. I was sick of avoiding all I needed to face by shopping more or delving into fantasies of being with George Clooney (yes, really). I am an original George Clooney fan from *The Facts of Life, ER,* heck, I was even obsessed with him in *Batman.* George is the only celebrity I have ever loved (well, there was Danny from *New Kids on The Block,* but the love of George Clooney has sustained me for most of my life.) When my husband and I would fight, when the reality of my days felt too unbearable, I would just close my eyes and drift off to my alternative universe with George. But even fantasies of George were not going to sustain me through the rest of my life.

Day after day, year after year, I made the decision to be in this relationship, to play small to lose myself and what I desired and deserved. That is all on me. I accept that. Now, I can also make the decision to step out of it too. I could make a decision to pick me. I could make a decision to live an extraordinary life of my own choosing, rather than just trying to survive the life I was in now.

And that is exactly what I did.

I wiped the tears and snot streaming down my face and I decided, right then and there, that I wouldn't wake up at 50 feeling the same way. Something was going to change. I didn't know what. I certainly didn't know how. But this uninspired, incompatible, mundane life was killing me slowly. And I didn't want to die. I wanted to live courageously, completely and authentically as all of me in every possible way.

I stood up from the floor of my closet and slipped back into my bed. As I laid there, I felt profound gratitude for being in that moment so fully and so completely. I was so grateful for the awareness of this moment. Yet, I also felt the fear of what would happen next.

"Do you think you can do any better, Beeki," my mom said to me over the phone.

Beeki was the name only my Mom and Dad called me. I was only five or six years old when the name stuck. Beeker was my favorite character on The Muppet Show. He mumbled. I also mumbled. While watching the show together, they would both lovingly call me Beeker. Beeker slowly became Beeki. And well, 40-plus years later, it is still what I was being called.

"Mom, I just hate living like this." I said it almost pleadingly.

It was one of many conversations between my mom and I on my marriage. I needed to get her on board, and in my corner if I was going to walk away from this.

She didn't understand my marriage.

How could she?

She and my Dad had 30 years and four months of pure magic before my dad's life was tragically cut short.

My Dad always felt like he had won the arranged marriage lottery. He was a simple farmer back in India. My mom was a beauty queen from the big city. Every time he saw my mom—whether it was simply coming home from work or seeing her across a crowded room at a party – his face would light up. The twinkle in his eye became extra-activated. He loved my mom. He loved her strength, her grace, her poise. He loved how she made our life seem extraordinary and beautiful even when there were financial hardships.

Mom loved Dad too. The way he made her laugh. His devotion to his family. The hyper present and super committed father he was to his three kids. But mostly, she loved and respected his strength. To work so hard, day in and day out, just to provide for all of us.

It was a marriage of respect, of love, of companionship, of laughter and fun. My siblings and I saw them at the best of times and the worst of times. But no matter what life threw their way, they handled it together as a team.

My marriage was the opposite and my mom knew it too. Just like my girlfriends, she got countless calls from me sharing complaints of my marriage. And even without me telling her she always knew when something was wrong the way Moms do.

But now I had a little girl, and my mom was terrified that I was going to tear up this life in the hopes that a new one would be better. I was scared too. I was stepping into unknown territory and I certainly didn't know how it would all unfold either.

What will happen to your little girl?

Do you really want her to be a product of a broken home?

Are you really going to do this to her and mess up her life?

These thoughts were not just those of my Mom's, although she was unrelenting in voicing them. They were mine too. The idea of my daughter's upbringing being so different from my own was completely foreign to me. Maybe I should keep living in this uninspired, loveless, hamster wheel just to keep things stable for her? After all, there were always my George Clooney fantasies to get me through my days. *Sigh.* These thoughts were constantly zipping around in my mind. I couldn't escape the enormity that my decision to not be in this marriage may have on my daughter.

One day, I was sipping my morning coffee in my backyard, admiring my roses and watching the hummingbirds zip around from flower to flower. The water in the pool was twinkling as the sun's warm rays beamed down. It was my favorite part of my day. Just to sip my coffee slowly, before my husband and daughter woke up, and just admired the view. I would get lost in my thoughts and the most beautiful epiphanies would emerge.

That is when this *a-ha* moment landed clear as day.

My daughter's upbringing was already profoundly different from my own. She had two parents who barely spoke with each other. She had parents who didn't share their meals together. She had parents who showed no love or admiration for the other in front of her (or privately). She had two parents who were living completely divergent lives just under one roof.

How could this be good for my daughter?

What is she learning watching her mom play small?

What is she learning from a father who is disinterested in her mom?

What is she learning from a mom disgusted by her dad?

What is she learning watching her parents not interact with each other on anything other than logistics of caring for her?

Keeping her in this life was far more damaging than removing her from this.

Up until this moment I believed I was doing something that would mess her up, ruin her life, that she would be destroyed from it forever. But at this moment, I realized separating from this life, this marriage, and creating a two-home structure was not messing her up. It was lifting her up. She would finally experience a life where both of her parents are thriving in their respective homes and solely focused on giving her the very best of themselves.

Yes, I already made the decision that I couldn't continue to live this way. But now, at this moment, I fully accept that this decision was not only good for me, but it would be the best possible outcome for my daughter too. No matter what anyone said to me, no matter what cultural belief they threw at me, no matter what slur was levied, I knew in my bones this decision was right for all of us.

As I sat on the deck in my backyard, I became overwhelmed with emotion. Through the tears, this phrase emerged:

Universe, show me the way.

The realizations had all hit. I knew it was what needed to happen. But I was paralyzed in terms of what action to take. Days, weeks, and months went by and the enormity of the decision weighed on me. Would it be like the movies where the lead character packs up and leaves with her child, never to be seen again? No, that felt too dramatic and too unnecessary. As much as I didn't want to live a life with my husband, I didn't hate him. He was a good dad and loved his daughter.

Universe, show me the way.

Maybe we could talk about it and mutually agree that we are better apart. Kinda like Gwyneth Paltrow and Chris Martin, who decided to consciously uncouple, remain friends, and still be a working family unit while not married, and not living together anymore. No, that isn't likely either. Someone who lacked self-awareness and nothing wrong in this marriage or continuing to live this way wasn't going to be able to consciously uncouple

Universe, show me the way.

In the end, he filed for divorce against me. I think it was a threat. Like he was saying, look what I am capable of if you don't straighten out and just stay in this thing. *"It's just a piece of paper."* He said to me after I was served with the divorce documents, grinning from ear to ear. As if the divorce papers were the equivalent to junk mail you just toss in the trash.

And so it began.

A contentious divorce. Lies. Deceit. Trickery. Pain, Hurt. Sadness. Ups and down of a legal process that I knew nothing about and never want to be part of again. Money burning in a lengthy and seemingly unnecessary fight. Two years of living in fear of what would happen next. What allegation would be levied. What pain would need to be endured. What shock to the system was coming next.

Each day through it all, I continued to pray the same prayer.

Universe, show me the way.

And at each step it did. Universe showed me the way to ME. Each time I entered a courtroom, was berated with demeaning or threatening texts, each time I was subject to the glares of his friends, and the whispers of my extended family gossiping with delight, each time I saw my accounts dwindle to nothing, not knowing how the next step was even possible, the nights my daughter was with her dad, adjusting to her new two-home set up, and I cried in utter defeat waiting for her to be back with me again, I was releasing the layers of this marriage.

I was releasing each moment I tried to make it work.

I was releasing each moment I accepted less than I deserved.

I was releasing each moment of playing small.

I was releasing each moment of a life that looked good on the outside but was diminishing me slowly on the inside.

And wow, did the Universe deliver.

Today, life is extraordinary in every way. My daughter and I are thriving. Abundance and prosperity is following us at every turn. We are both magnets for the most beautiful experiences this life has to offer. And we are both living a life we love. A life that is full, engaging, inspiring, love filled and extraordinary in every possible way.

There is no lack.

There is no sadness for the life we left behind.

There is only so much profound gratitude for all of life's experiences that brought me to this moment.

Walking a red carpet and receiving a literary award for my own story that is inspiring the world to believe more in themselves and all that is truly possible.

That's why I wore red tonight.

I want to be seen.

Look at me, Universe.

I am here.

I did it.

On the red carpet, a reporter turned her microphone toward me and asked, *"Congratulations on your award tonight, Deepika. Tell me, what inspired your book?"*

I looked at her and smiled, *"How much time do you have?"*

Deepika is the CEO of Soul Sparks Press, a four-time award-winning, best-selling author, TV show host, retired Silicon Valley Business Executive, and Mom. Deepika has inspired more than 20,000 people worldwide through her books, speaking, thought leadership, courses, and one-on-one private mentorship. Deepika's debut book *Hello Universe, It's Me* garnered literary acclaim as a 2024 Critically Acclaimed Best Seller by the LA Tribune and as the winner of the 2023 Silver Prize at the Nautilus Book Awards.

Deepika lives in the San Francisco Bay Area with her sweet and sassy pre-teen daughter and their new puppy.

Connect with Deepika on Instagram @deepikasandhu.co or LinkedIn at https://www.linkedin.com/in/deepikasandhu/.

EPILOGUE

Dear brave reader,

As you close this book of twelve inspiring journeys, I want you to meet someone extraordinary: your future self. I am you, but a version you might find hard to recognize right now. I'm the woman who emerged from the ashes of divorce, stronger and more vibrant than ever before.

Let me tell you what you have in store.

A life you might not yet believe is possible.

Even after reading these stories of women just like you, who moved out of a bad marriage, you may still be doubting yourself, thinking, "Well this is them. It won't work for me."

If that is you, I want you to stop doubting yourself, questioning yourself, and Sis, I want you to stop putting your needs and desires last.

Those days are behind you now.

I want you to wake up each morning and remember YOU ARE THE PRIZE. You deserve to take up space. You can do it. I believe in you. Yes, you!

Now, when I start my day, I look in the mirror and genuinely smile at the woman I see. A woman who's weathered storms and came out stronger and more vibrant because of it.

I went from a woman who was scared to a woman who moves through the world with a confidence I once thought impossible. I voice my opinions without second-guessing myself, I make decisions – big and small – trusting my own judgment. The paralyzing fear of rejection that once held me back, has transformed into a quiet self-assurance. I no longer shrink myself to fit others' expectations. Instead, I stand tall, speak my truth, and own my worth.

Yes, some friends and family took a step back during those dark days of divorce. But, my support system has expanded in ways I never imagined possible. I've cultivated deep, meaningful friendships with women who truly see and appreciate me. We lift each other up, celebrating our wins and hold space for the fears, sadness, and tough days. I've found a community that reminds me daily that I am not alone.

Speaking of not being alone – once I learned to stand on my own two feet and that I was deserving of this new life I desired, my dream man walked into my life. Let me tell you, I now have a love that has shown me what true emotional safety feels like. He respects my independence and celebrates my successes as if they were his own. Our conflicts, instead of driving us apart, become opportunities for growth that actually bring us closer together. We face challenges head-on, neither of us run when things get tough.

What is most beautiful is our unwavering commitment to each other and to our relationship. I never question whether he loves me, because he shows me every single day.

This isn't a fairy tale romance with grand gestures and unrealistic expectations. It's a love grounded in truth—deep, authentic, and built on a foundation of mutual respect and admiration. He sees me fully—strengths, flaws, and everything in between—and loves every part, even the messy bits. And in his eyes, I see a reflection of my own worth that I once struggled to recognize.

Remember how you used to settle for crumbs of affection? Now, I experience affection in abundance, daily. I've learned that true love begins with self-love, and that's a well that never runs dry as long as I keep prioritizing it.

I've rediscovered passions I had forgotten, and uncovered new ones I never knew existed. Last month, I took a solo trip to Bali—something I'd always dreamed of but never dared to do. The old me would have found a dozen reasons why it wasn't possible. The new me booked the ticket and had the adventure of a lifetime.

I've learned to dream bigger, to reach higher. That book idea you've been thinking about? I'm halfway through writing it. That career change you've been considering? I made the leap, and it was the best decision ever. I've realized that life expands in proportion to our courage.

Here's the most beautiful part—I've become a beacon of hope for others. Women often approach me, drawn by my light of true joy. They ask, "How did you do it?" And I smile, remembering the journey, remembering you—where it all began.

So, my dear past self, here's what I want you to know:

1. The pain you feel now is sculpting you into a masterpiece. It will propel you into the life that brings you so much joy.
2. Your intuition is your superpower. Trust it fiercely.
3. Self-love isn't selfish—it's your birthright. Prioritize it & give to others from the overflow.
4. Your dreams aren't too big—your thinking might be too small. Expand it.
5. The right people will love you for exactly who you are. Accept nothing less.

The journey from where you are to where I am wasn't always easy. Giving up and staying in what you know can feel more than tempting. It often feels easier than the fear we have about new choices, a new life. But I promise you, every tear, every moment of self-doubt, every brave step forward—it's all worth it.

You have within you everything you need to create a life that surpasses your wildest dreams. Trust in your journey, invest in yourself, and be open to support along the way. I'm cheering you on, knowing the incredible transformation that awaits you.

I have immense belief in you.

Love,

Your Happy Future Self

After navigating divorce in her 30s and finding profound love on her own terms, **Shilpa Cacho** now guides women to attract their soul-husbands through deep, lasting transformation. Her whole-person methodology, informed by her background in psychology and occupational therapy, combines practical dating strategies with mind-body-soul work. Shilpa takes pride in helping women not only find love but become the most authentic, magnetic versions of themselves – breaking free from people-pleasing patterns and creating soul-level partnerships that expand their lives. Through her unique integration of practical and spiritual approaches, she helps women develop unshakeable self-trust and the ability to attract (not chase) the deep love they desire.

SCAN HERE TO
LEARN MORE ABOUT